CHALLENGE BOXES

50 Projects in Creative Thinking

☆ ☆ ☆ ☆ ☆ ☆ ☆ Grades 4-8, gifted

Catherine Slough Valentino

DALE
SEYMOUR
PUBLICATIONS
P.O. BOX 10888
PALO ALTO, CA 94303

THANK YOU . . .

to the teachers and administrators in North Kingstown whose libraries, halls, classrooms, and windowsills are cluttered with colorful boxes.

to all my friends and colleagues who badgered me until I submitted the Challenge Boxes for publication.

to Martha Hough and Mary Hargraves, who devoted time to getting the program started and keeping boxes filled.

to Dr. Marge Bumpus, my educational idol and dear friend, who gave me an A+ on the original set of Challenge Boxes in a graduate reading course.

to Dom, who mailed out hundreds of Challenge Boxes books back in the good ol' days.

to Nick and Benji, my biggest and most beloved fan club.

Illustrations: Dennis Nolan
Cover design: John Edeen

ISBN 0-86651-130-X

Order number DS07321   efghi-MA-898

CONTENTS

PREFACE

The majority of students labeled "academically talented" (for practical purposes, those who score in the eightieth percentile and above on standardized achievement tests) can and must be serviced within the regular classroom. While curriculum compacting and help from a resource room are important in a program for gifted students, the greater part of any student's time is generally spent in a heterogeneously grouped classroom. The regular classroom teacher's attention to the individual difference we call "gifted" is essential. The Challenge Boxes program can help. In one sense, this program is as much dedicated to increasing the commitment of the classroom teacher to gifted students as it is to improving such students' thinking skills.

These Challenge Boxes reflect several underlying assumptions about programs for the gifted. First, academically talented students in public schools need opportunities to *integrate* the subjects they study, both creatively and productively. Thinking-skills programs currently on the market stress brainstorming, fluency, flexibility, and originality, but they stop short of helping students transfer those skills to curriculum content areas. The Challenge Boxes are specifically designed to provide that experience.

Second, programs for academically talented students need to encourage independent thinking through highly *motivating* activities. Too often, programs for the gifted simply involve difficult and tedious research or lengthy problems from which a student's only satisfaction is the completion of the activity itself. The Challenge Boxes avoid that problem with imaginative activities that students respond to with genuine enthusiasm.

Finally, keep in mind that giftedness is not a quality or a set of behaviors that above-average students either *have* or *don't have*. Rather, it is part of a continuum of individual differences in students. Selection into a gifted program should be determined to a great extent by a student's performance in the activities of that program, not just by the student's achievement and aptitude test scores. In other words, if the program is properly designed, it will be self-selecting. Just as your students' placement in a higher reading group is determined by their reading skills, so should your students' involvement in the Challenge Boxes program depend on their performance on their first Challenge Box projects.

PART 1   INTRODUCTION

CHALLENGE BOXES: AN OVERVIEW

"Challenge Boxes" is a program that was started in the North Kingstown, Rhode Island public schools in 1980. Based on a collection of mind-stretching projects designed to stimulate bright students in grades 4-8, this program represents a clear and vigorous response to the charge that today's academically talented students aren't being sufficiently challenged in the classroom.

This *Challenge Boxes* book is an outgrowth of that highly successful program. It contains fifty of the most popular and demanding projects developed for that program, projects that cross over a variety of curriculum areas: science, language arts, social studies, math, art.

The projects in this book focus on higher level thinking skills and encourage student creativity in curriculum content areas. The emphasis is also on *productive* thinking: students may be asked to invent something (a bubble machine, a water clock), to critically evaluate and improve the performance of something else (a balsa airplane), to analyze how something works (a Coke machine, a battery), or to produce their own version of something they have analyzed (the special effects in King Kong).

Other projects require students to analyze data and draw conclusions based on that analysis. In "Umwelt," for example, students read *The View from the Oak,* a book that describes the sensory capabilities of a wide variety of animals. They analyze the information and apply it by reproducing (artistically) a natural scene as it would appear to three separate animals. For this and most of the boxes, there is no one "right" answer; student responses will vary widely according to the interest, thought, and creativity they invest in the project.

Group discussions after students have successfully completed a Challenge Box project are an important part of the program. Listening and responding to the ideas of others helps students evaluate their work, gain new insights into problems, and refine and expand their own thinking skills.

The Challenge Box activities often ignite a student's interest in other related topics. Such a student is encouraged to undertake independent projects under the guidance of the classroom or resource-room teacher. Additionally, students are often eager to create their own Challenge Boxes on themes of special interest to them. For instance, one student invented a box she called "Cancel It Out," asking students to identify the source of twenty foreign postage stamps and label the countries on a blank world map. Properly done, student-created boxes like this one can be shared successfully throughout the school.

WHY BOXES?

From the beginning, boxes have been an integral part of the program. The author first used shoe boxes donated by a local shoe distributor, but later found a better answer: brightly colored 9″ × 12″ × 3″ boxes with hinged lids, deep enough to hold reference books and materials, and just wide enough to keep notebooks and papers flat and tidy. While any of the projects *could* be done without them, the boxes offer several distinct advantages:

☆ Putting each project in a box contains the problem for the child, psychologically as well as physically.

☆ For class management, the boxes help a teacher keep together the instructions, task cards, pictures, books, maps, and any other items that constitute the "starter materials" for each project.

☆ The boxes are a convenient and colorful way to store the projects in the classroom, library, or media center, on shelves or on tables. Students can easily check them out, like books, for independent work.

☆ Students use the box as a means of storage and organization for the books, notes, art materials, and other items they use as they work on the project. (Those who are familiar with the usual state of 9- to 13-year-olds' desks and rooms will appreciate this feature.)

☆ Finally, the boxes add an element of mysterious fascination, even sophistication, to the project: the idea of carrying around a box labeled "Bones," or "Clandestine," or "Wonder Blob," has undeniable appeal for middle-grade students.

STUDENT SELECTION

How you select students to participate in the Challenge Boxes program will vary, depending on how you choose to set up and run the program. We offer three basic recommendations regarding student selection:

1. Student performance should always be a major factor in the selection process. The Challenge Boxes can be used initially as exploratory enrichment activities in the general classroom, without a formal selection procedure. Allow all students access to the projects; the difficulty of the material will serve as a self-selecting device. That is, students who are unable to complete a box successfully will usually show a lack of interest in further activities.

2. If you choose to institute a pull-out program, you will need some measure of academic achievement or ability since the Challenge Boxes involve extended work in the basic curriculum areas.

3. Parents should be involved in some real way when you are gathering data about their children for the selection process. This program encourages parent participation, and involving them from the beginning will help elicit their cooperation and ensure their understanding of the program.

THE THREE-STEP PROGRAM

The Challenge Boxes program is set up so that students may proceed through three steps, depending on their performance and interest:

Step One   Completing a Box
Step Two   Follow-up Discussion
Step Three   Independent Study Project

Within this general outline, there are many options for managing the program.

Step One: Completing a Box

How do the students obtain a box, and who will evaluate the students' work once they have completed their projects? Here are some of the alternatives:

☆ Students check out boxes in the regular classroom to complete in their free time, as part of their class assignments or as homework.

☆ The librarian or media specialist handles the procedures involved in checking out the boxes and keeps records of each box a student has completed. A student's classroom teacher evaluates the boxes initially.

☆ Students check the boxes out of their individual classrooms, and a team of teachers in the school meets periodically to evaluate student products.

☆ Students check the boxes out of a media center or library, and a team of teachers evaluates the products. Or . . .

☆ Students check the boxes out of a media center or library, and the librarian evaluates the projects and summarizes the results for classroom teachers.

☆ The classroom teacher is relieved by a substitute one day per month, using this day to meet with and evaluate the products of the students in his or her class.

☆ The classroom teacher chooses one box as a class project for all students and sets aside thirty minutes of class time for students to share their products and evaluate the results.

Step Two: Follow-up Discussion

While the Challenge Boxes may be used simply as individual enrichment activities in the classroom, their value is enhanced when you use the results to spark group discussions, debate, and evaluation by peers. Following are several options for organizing group discussions among students who have all successfully completed the same Challenge Box:

☆ An individual teacher groups such students for discussion within the regular classroom.

☆ Teachers with expertise in a particular area arrange to guide the discussion of certain Challenge Boxes for students either at a single grade level or across grade levels. Ideally this option involves only a small number of students, ten or fewer per group.

☆ A team of teachers handles the scheduling of group discussions in conjunction with a resource teacher.

☆ A resource-room specialist arranges and guides the discussion of Challenge Boxes as a part of the regular resource-room program.

☆ A media specialist or librarian meets with students to discuss the projects and encourage the sharing of ideas.

☆ The school principal meets with small groups of students who have successfully completed a Challenge Box. If a principal has the background, desire, and time to participate in this program, the rewards are great. Positive community response is overwhelming. Furthermore, the principal gets the chance to be involved with students that for the most part he or she seldom sees. (Regardless of the principal's role in this step of the Challenge Boxes program, administrative support is essential to its success.)

☆ Parents with expertise in a given area meet with students to provide feedback and facilitate group discussion.

☆ An after-school Challenge Box club is formed, and students themselves control the checking-out and discussion of boxes under an elected group leader.

Step Three: Independent Study Project

When a Challenge Box acts as an appetizer, whetting a student's appetite for more knowledge on a given topic, that student will often be motivated to delve into independent study and research.

Following are some of the options for handling this:

☆ The classroom teacher and the interested student arrange the independent study project as part of the child's classroom work. Usually, routine work is eliminated or reduced while the student works on the independent project. A librarian may assist the student.

☆ A resource teacher, in consultation with the classroom teacher, is responsible for directing the independent study projects.

☆ A team of teachers meets to identify areas or subjects in which each might function as a resource to a small number of students involved in a particular project.

☆ High school students with a strong background in one area are brought in to advise students on their independent study projects.

☆ Community members serve as advisors and guides to students who become involved in an area related to their expertise.

☆ Parents of interested students provide assistance with the independent projects.

☆ The students themselves take a large role in planning their own independent projects and also make the effort to assist each other.

Sometimes an independent study project can be turned into a new Challenge Box that can be shared with other students in the program. Students who are interested in this idea should follow the ground rules on the "Design a Challenge Box" sheet and model their boxes after those already in use.

PROJECT FORMAT AND USE

Whether you prefer to institute the entire Challenge Boxes program or simply want to use selected projects for enrichment, you will need materials from Part 2 of this book. Following is a description of what you will find to help you set up the program and each of the projects in it.

Project Selection Guide

An annotated list of the 50 projects appears on pages 9-11. This summary of what each project is all about is a useful guide as you familiarize yourself with the contents of the program.

Project Masters

Beginning on page 13, you will find blackline-master materials to duplicate and cut apart in order to assemble the boxes. Some projects are complete in a single page; others have follow-up pages that may include task cards, response sheets, and sample answers or answer guidelines. Any page may be duplicated.

Master copies of all the sheets pertaining to a single project should be kept together in a master reference file. Consumable pages (such as response sheets) can be duplicated in larger quantities and kept on file for easy replacement when a box is returned.

Every project opens on a new page like this:

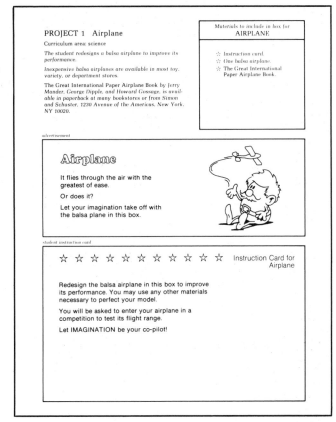

Project overview

Materials to assemble for the project.

Advertisement

Student instruction card

Project overview. This tells you the curriculum content areas involved in the project and offers a summary of what the student is asked to do. The overview also includes ordering information for books and maps that are listed as starter materials.

The materials list. This lists all the items (sometimes there are options) that you need to include in the box. Whoever is responsible for managing the program should keep a copy of each materials list, either with the box iteself or in a convenient file. Whenever one student returns a box, the materials list should be reviewed to be sure everything is there before the box is made available for check-out again.

The advertisement. This is a tool to motivate students and to interest them in doing a project. The ads can be duplicated, colored, and placed on the side or top of a Challenge Box to attract attention and advertise what's inside. They might also be backed with colored paper and used to create a bulletin board or wall display advertising the Challenge Boxes program. One librarian made banners with the ads copied on them and hung these around the media center. Students could be enlisted to help in such an effort.

The student instruction card. This card is to be duplicated, cut out, and placed inside each Challenge Box. The instruction card can be permanently affixed to the inside cover of the box with rubber cement, or can be laminated and left loose inside with the other materials. A master copy of this card should always be kept on file for the teacher's reference.

Follow-up pages. When task cards, response sheets, or other specialty pieces are part of a project, they are found immediately following the project-opening page. Each is clearly labeled with the project name. Instructions for their preparation are given in the project overview. Again, master copies of these items should be kept on file.

Sample answer pages. With some projects you will find samples of actual student responses. These are *not* model answers; they are *not* a standard by which to judge your own students' work. Rather, they are included simply to give you a frame of reference, and a taste of the kind of creative responses you can expect. Occasionally you may find that a student fails to follow the instructions to the letter, but nonetheless submits a thoughtful and creative project. In evaluating such student work, always remember that the final goal is creative and productive thinking.

Materials to Purchase

Eighteen of the projects require starter materials—books, maps, or everyday objects like aluminum foil that you may already have on hand. While these items are listed with each project, you may want to use this comprehensive list (page 115) to help you assemble the needed materials. It lists the materials by project, with addresses for special-ordering items not readily available in local stores.

The Want Ads

The advertisements for all 50 Challenge Boxes are included together, sometimes in a shortened form, on two pages called "The Want Ads" (pages 117-118). These can be used by students to decide which project appeals to them; one master copy might be laminated and kept on display or on file wherever the boxes are stored. The Want Ads can also serve as individual record-keeping forms, with each student keeping his or her own copy and marking off projects as they are completed.

Certificate of Independent Study

This certificate (page 119) can be duplicated on a heavier or nicer paper stock, then filled out and awarded to students who have completed a pre-determined number of Challenge Boxes (ten, for example).

Design a Challenge Box

Students who have completed and discussed one or more Challenge Boxes and have begun independent study projects (Step Three) are sometimes interested in developing Challenge Boxes of their own. This brief instruction sheet (page 120) offers simple guidelines for such an undertaking.

Sample Letters to Parents

As indicated earlier, parent interest and involvement has always been a valuable part of the Challenge Boxes program. These sample letters (pages 121-122) can serve as models for letters you write yourself, describing your particular use of the Challenge Boxes and encouraging parental cooperation.

THE UNWRITTEN RULES

1. A student may ask ANYONE in the world for information leading to the completion of a Challenge Box, EXCEPT his or her teacher and school librarian.

2. Parents are enthusiastically invited to join in the fun and to get involved with a child's activity.

3. While some projects are harder than others (because they vary in the amount of literal, creative, and theoretical thinking they require), the Challenge Boxes themselves are not color-coded to indicate levels of difficulty. Students select boxes because of their interest in the activity.

4. Although the Challenge Boxes are designed for individual use, they can be done with an entire class of students as well; all that's required is extra copies of the student instruction card and other necessary materials.

5. Students may work together as partners on a Challenge Box. They then divide the credit (one credit per box) by the number of students who worked together.

6. Any student completing ten Challenge Boxes (or another number determined by the teacher) receives a Certificate of Independent Study.

7. There is no recommended time limit for doing most of the Challenge Boxes, although a teacher may choose to set one.

PART 2   THE 50 PROJECTS

PROJECT SELECTION GUIDE

PROJECT 1 Airplane

Curriculum area: science

The student redesigns a balsa airplane to improve its performance.

Inexpensive balsa airplanes are available in most toy, variety, or department stores.

The Great International Paper Airplane Book by Jerry Mander, George Dipple, and Howard Gossage, is available in paperback at many bookstores or from Simon and Schuster, 1230 Avenue of the Americas, New York, NY 10020.

advertisement

Airplane

It flies through the air with the greatest of ease.

Or does it?

Let your imagination take off with the balsa plane in this box.

student instruction card

Instruction Card for Airplane

Redesign the balsa airplane in this box to improve its performance. You may use any other materials necessary to perfect your model.

You will be asked to enter your airplane in a competition to test its flight range.

Let IMAGINATION be your co-pilot!

PROJECT 2   At Your Convenience

Curriculum areas: science, language arts, reference skills

Faced with the hypothetical disappearance of several modern conveniences, the student researches three and describes the appearance, the manufacture, and the workings of each for the benefit of future generations.

The convenience items listed for inclusion in the box are available at most variety stores, pharmacies, or department stores.

One set of sample student answers is included on page 15 for your reference.

advertisement

At Your Convenience

These modern-day conveniences could disappear
forever . . . unless YOU can remember how they worked.

student instruction card

Instruction Card for
At Your Convenience

The items in this box will disappear from the earth
forever in just seven days. You have exactly that long
to figure out how they work so that you can reinvent them.

Choose any three of the conveniences you find in the box.
For posterity, describe in writing what each item looks
like, how it was made, and how it works.

PROJECT 2   At Your Convenience
Sample student answer

The sample below is the response of one student who chose the match, the battery, and the light bulb. This is for your reference only; it is NOT an answer key.

1. MATCHES

Definition: A short, slim piece of wood or cardboard which is tipped with a mixture by which it can be ignited by friction.

Manufacturing: The wood or paper for the splints must be cut to proper size, dipped to create heads, and assembled in books or boxes to be sold. The tip is made from antimony sulphide, potassium chlorate, gum, and starch. The friction when the match is struck causes it to light. Book matches usually have a surface on them for the match to be struck on.

2. BATTERY

Definition: A device that produces electricity by means of a chemical reaction.

The battery consists of one or more units called electrical cells. Each cell has all the parts needed to produce an electrical current. There are various kinds of batteries. The design of the battery determines the amount of electricity provided. Some batteries are called primary batteries and stop working. Other batteries are called secondary or storage batteries and can be recharged. The battery contained in this box is a primary battery. It has two structures called electrodes. An electrolyte between the electrodes causes one of them, called an anode, to become negatively charged and the other one, called a cathode, to become positively charged.

Manufacturing: The battery is contained in a zinc can. This can serves as both a container for the parts of the battery and as an anode. There is a carbon rod in the center which functions as the cathode current collector, but the actual cathode material is a mixture of manganese dioxide and carbon powder that is packed around the sod. The electrolyte is a paste composed of ammonium chloride, zinc chloride, and water. The anode and the cathode are separated by cardboard, soaked with the electrolyte. This thin layer is used to prevent the electrode materials from mixing together.

3. THE ELECTRIC LIGHT BULB

A light bulb has three major parts: the filament, the bulb, and the base. The filament is a thin coil of wire found in the bulb. Electricity flows through it when the lamp is on. The filament gives resistance to the electricity. To overcome the resistance it must heat up to 4500°F. This high temperature makes the filament glow and give off light.

The bulb's purpose is to keep air away from the filament to prevent it from burning up. Most bulbs contain a mixture of gases instead of air, usually argon and nitrogen. Manufacturers coat the inside of the bulb with silica or cut it with acid. The base has two main purposes. It holds the lamp in its fixture and it connects the lamp to the electrical current.

—Eileen

PROJECT 3   Audubon

Curriculum areas: art, reference skills

The student explores the world of art and art history, finding twenty paintings that contain birds, identifying the artist and year of completion for each work, and judging which artist is the closest "runner-up" to John James Audubon.

advertisement

Audubon

This box is for the birds . . .
and for you, too, if you like your
friends fine and feathered.

student instruction card

Instruction Card for
Audubon

Audubon isn't the only artist whose canvases depict a bird or two.

1. Fill this box with the titles of twenty paintings
   (not necessarily by the same artists) that contain
   one or more birds. For each painting, list the artist
   and the year in which the work was completed.

2. Nominate an artist as runner-up to Audubon in capturing
   the essence of mankind's fine-feathered friends.

PROJECT 4   Believe It or Not

Curriculum areas: math, language arts

The student explores the realm of probability, coming up with and testing ten statements that are true 50 percent of the time and false 50 percent of the time.

advertisement

Believe It or Not

Six of one, half a dozen of the other.

If you are able to see both sides of
a problem, you are assured of at least
a 50 percent chance of completing this box.

student instruction card

Instruction Card for
Believe It or Not

Fill this box with ten statements that are TRUE
approximately 50 percent of the time and
FALSE approximately 50 percent of the time.

PROJECT 5   Big Foot

Curriculum areas: language arts, science, social studies

After analyzing the threat Big Foot might pose to a group camping trip, the student selects appropriate data and opinions to put together a list of persuasive arguments either for (Task Card A) or against (Task Card B) such a trip. The student must further judge the arguments and rank them from strongest to weakest.

advertisement

Big Foot

Would you go camping alone in the wilds of Northern California and Oregon?

Try this box and then decide.

student instruction card

   Instruction Card for Big Foot

Big Foot has been variously described as a great undiscovered ape or a descendant of primitive man. Descriptions from self-proclaimed eyewitnesses maintain that the creature stands about seven feet tall, has a hairy body with strong thick arms and big feet, stands erect, and is usually found near water in mountainous areas.

Researchers cannot agree on the existence of Big Foot as a specific being or species. They do agree, however, that no one has proved that Big Foot does *not* exist.

To complete this box, read the task card and prepare a convincing argument.

Big Foot

Your class is planning an extensive camping trip in Northern California this summer. The trip, however, is in jeopardy, because of the possibility that Big Foot might be encountered in the camping area. Not enough parents have signed permission slips allowing their children to go on the trip.

The chairman of the School Trip Committee has called a meeting. You have been asked to prepare a statement that will change the mind of the concerned parents. Success in dealing with these parents will depend on the strength of your logic. Do your best! Without the trip, your summer could be a bust.

Number your arguments and list them in order from strongest to weakest.

Task Card A

Big Foot

Your class is planning an extensive camping trip in Northern California this summer. You are not excited, however, because you have premonitions of disaster.

You must convince your parents *not* to sign the permission slip allowing you to accompany your class. Your success in dealing with your parents will depend on the strength of your logic. Do your best! Your life may depend on it.

Number your arguments and list them in order from strongest to weakest.

Task Card B

PROJECT 6   Big Mac

Curriculum areas: science, social studies

Turning the mundane into something ingenious; turning a throwaway into something useful—that's the goal of this project. The student uses five styrofoam hamburger boxes to make a magic trick, something to take camping, and something helpful in an emergency.

advertisement

Big Mac

Next time you have a Big Mac attack, save the styrofoam container.

It will come in handy if you are able to attack the problem in this box successfully.

student instruction card

Instruction Card for Big Mac

Use the styrofoam hamburger containers in this box to construct the following items:

1. A magic trick.
2. A useful item to take on a camping trip.
3. Something to use in an emergency. (You must name the emergency.)

PROJECT 7 Bones

Curriculum areas: science, reference skills

The student does research as needed to determine what skeletal features of various animals are necessary for making the eight different movements listed on the task card. The student then combines these representative features in a single imaginary animal that can make all the movements, creating either a picture or a model of its complete skeletal system.

One sample of student work is included on page 23 for your reference.

advertisement

Bones

Make no bones about it! Some animals can fly, some can hang by their tails, and some can peel bananas. If you mix up the bones, who knows what an animal could do!

Complete this box and you'll have an animal that can do all three and more.

student instruction card

Instruction Card for Bones

Prepare a picture or model of the skeletal system of an imaginary animal that can perform the feats listed on the task card.

Bones

Your goal is to create an animal that can do all eight of the following:

1. Hop.
2. Fly for short distances.
3. Hang by its tail.
4. Look over its shoulder.
5. Peel a banana.
6. Climb a tree.
7. Stand erect.
8. Eat raw chickens.

 Task Card

PROJECT 7   Bones
Sample student answer

The sample below is just one student's idea and should not be considered an answer key.

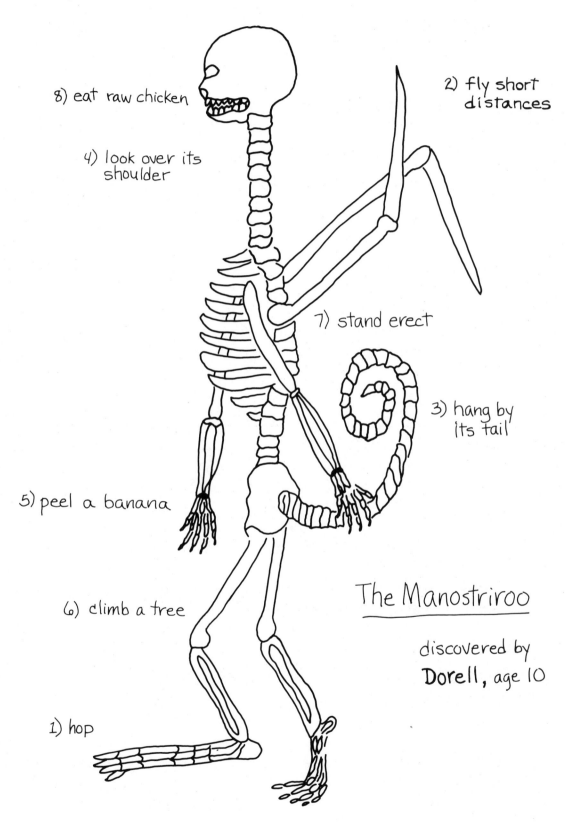

8) eat raw chicken

2) fly short distances

4) look over its shoulder

7) stand erect

3) hang by its tail

5) peel a banana

6) climb a tree

The Manostriroo

discovered by Dorell, age 10

1) hop

PROJECT 8 Boomerang

Curriculum areas: language arts, science

Leaving plenty of room for imagination and humor, this project asks the student to find twenty items (pictures, models, or descriptions are also allowed) that will return faithfully, and to describe in one sentence how someone could prevent the return of each.

advertisement

Boomerang

This activity might come back to haunt you, especially if you sometimes find yourself running around in circles.

student instruction card

Instruction Card for Boomerang

Fling a boomerang into the sky and it will return—if it is properly constructed.

Fill this box with at least twenty objects (pictures, models, or descriptions are allowed) that will return faithfully.
For each item, give a one-sentence description of how you could prevent its return. For example:

A boomerang will always return *unless* it hits a kangaroo coming or going.

PROJECT 9 Boring

Curriculum areas: language arts, art

Everyone has been bored at one time or another—but why? What's boredom all about? How can it be avoided? The student explores the causes and effects of this common emotion and develops a philosophy of boredom, then makes a wall hanging or banner to reflect that philosophy.

Materials to include in box for
BORING

☆ *Instruction card.*

advertisement

Boring

Feeling bored? This box is a sure cure
for the doldrums. Or is it? After all,
as Einstein said, it's all relative.

student instruction card

Instruction Card for
Boring

1. Fill this box with the items listed on the task card.

2. Make a wall hanging or a paper banner that reflects or states your philosophy of boredom. Think about these questions:

   What is boredom?

   Why does it happen?

   Who are its victims?

   What are some remedies for it?

Boring

Fill this box with the following items.
And don't get too bored!

1. A picture of the most boring place on earth to be.
2. The title of the most boring book you have ever read. (Tell why it was boring.)
3. A description of the most tedious job you have ever done.
4. The word or words that describe the most monotonous sound you have ever heard.
5. The least exciting fact or concept you have ever learned.

Task Card

PROJECT 10 Bubble Box

Curriculum area: science

The student creates a bubble machine, choosing particular design features to emphasize either quantity (number of bubbles produced) or quality (size of bubbles produced).

For a lower level project include the optional "starter" materials, which can be found in most variety stores. For a higher level project, let students conceive and locate their own materials.

advertisement

Bubble Box

Lawrence Welk is forever blowing bubbles.

You will be, too, if you complete this box successfully!

student instruction card

☆ ☆ ☆ ☆ ☆ ☆ ☆ ☆ ☆ ☆ ☆   Instruction Card for Bubble Box

Design a bubble machine, using any materials you choose. You may have your machine judged in either of the following categories:

1. **Quantity.** Machine will be judged on the number of bubbles produced in a 30-second period.

2. **Quality.** Machine will be judged on the largest bubble produced in a 30-second period.

Indicate which category you prefer.

PROJECT 11 Clandestine

Curriculum area: language arts

The student conceives and describes a secret operation to disguise and transport twenty spacecraft to Washington, D.C., with the restriction that the craft cannot be completely enclosed.

Make a spacecraft for the box by covering a pop bottle cap with aluminum foil, stretching the foil to make a thin, smooth surface. Add windows around the sides with an indelible-ink marking pen.

advertisement

Clandestine

This box should prompt much DISCussion about how to DISCretely disguise an alien spacecraft. Don't get DISCouraged if you don't DISCover a solution immediately.

student instruction card

Instruction Card for Clandestine

Twenty small spacecraft exactly the size and shape of the one in this box land in your backyard. You are the only hope for the creatures who inhabit the craft. They are convinced that adults would eliminate them.

The creatures indicate to you that they have come in peace to communicate with the president of the United States. You must somehow disguise or camouflage all twenty spacecraft and transport them to Washington, D.C. You may not completely enclose the spaceships, because their supply of argon gleaned from Earth's atmosphere is limited, and without it the creatures would suffocate.

Describe in writing, or artistically, exactly how you would transport each spacecraft to the White House in Washington, D.C.

PROJECT 12   Coke Machine

Curriculum area: science

The student does research to answer a set of questions (Task Card A) about how a cold-drink dispenser works. Questions on Task Card B ask the student to analyze and classify the decision-making capabilities of such a machine.

One set of sample student answers is included on page 31 for your reference.

advertisement

Coke Machine

What happens when you put the money in a cold-drink dispenser?

We'll put in the questions; you dispense the answers!

student instruction card

Instruction Card for
Coke Machine

You put your money in, you push the button, and you get your drink. (Usually.)

The question is, what happens in between?

Answer the enclosed task-card questions, and then you'll know where the money goes.

Coke Machine

Suppose a Coke machine charges 45 cents a can.

1. What happens when you put in your 45 cents? How does the machine "know" you didn't put in 25 cents?

2. If you put in 50 cents, how does the Coke machine "know" how much change to return?

3. When you push the Pepsi button, why doesn't Fresca come out?

Task Card A

Coke Machine

Given that a Coke machine can make the "decisions" you explored on Task Card A:

1. Does the machine qualify as a computer? Why or why not?

2. Can it think? Why or why not?

Task Card B

PROJECT 12 Coke Machine
Sample student answer

The sample below, with the drawing on the following page, represents the response of one student to Task Cards A and B. This is for your reference only; it is NOT an answer key.

TASK CARD A

Suppose a Coke machine charges 45 cents a can.

1. *What happens when you put in your 45 cents? How does the machine "know" you didn't put in 25 cents?*

   It knows because of the coin(s) size, shape, and weight and if it is magnetic. The Coke machine has sensors to tell if the coin or coins are okay to pass on.

2. *If you put in 50 cents, how does the Coke machine "know" how much change to return?*

   It depends on what kind of Coke machine it is. If it is a computerized Coke machine it will weigh it and, knowing the weight, will then know how much change to return. The Coke machine that is not computerized will weigh the coins and, not knowing how much change to return, will simply return the money. Most non-computerized Coke machines require exact change.

3. *When you push the Pepsi button, why doesn't Fresca come out?**

   When you push the Coke button it releases a trigger that connects to the Coke compartment and it opens long enough so that one Coke comes out. It then travels down a funnel to the place that the Coke comes out.

TASK CARD B

Given that a Coke machine can make the "decisions" you explored on Task Card A:

1. *Does the machine qualify as a computer? Why or why not?*

   The Coke machine that is complicated and can return exact change would qualify as a computer. The Coke machine that is not complicated and requires exact change would not qualify as a computer.

2. *Can it think? Why or why not?*

   No, computers or non-computers can't think. People put the information in the computer and the computer uses what is in its memory bank.

One alert student pointed out that there would not be a Pepsi button because this is a Coke machine and Pepsi is not a product of Coca Cola corporation.

PROJECT 12   Coke Machine
Sample student answer

P.S. Since I can't explain exactly what happens, here is a picture of a Coke machine.

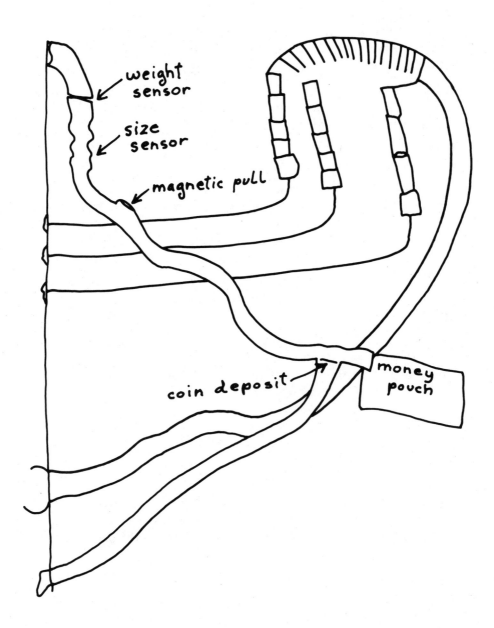

weight sensor

size sensor

magnetic pull

coin deposit

money pouch

—Sara, grade 5

PROJECT 13 Colorblind

Curriculum area: art

The student leaves the visual world and explores instead the tactile realm, creating a "rainbow" that represents an ordered range of textures.

advertisement

Colorblind

Have you ever touched a rainbow?

You'll find it a touching experience, once you get the feel for this "hands on" project.

student instruction card

Instruction Card for
Colorblind

Textures are as vivid and as varied to a blind person as colors are to a person with normal vision.

Design and construct a "rainbow" of textures that you feel best represents your world of touch. Remember that colors are *not* arranged randomly in a rainbow.

PROJECT 14   Dominoes

Curriculum area: math

The student performs experiments with different configurations of falling dominoes to answer the questions on the instruction card. This non-routine problem-solving situation calls on the student to decide on a solution strategy and to keep track of the results of experiments until a solution is found.

Dominoes can be purchased in most toy, variety, or department stores.

advertisement

Dominoes

The Domino Theory: if the first domino in a line falls, so do the rest.

Whether or not these dominoes fall along the lines of that theory rests with you.

student instruction card

☆ ☆ ★ ☆ ★ ☆ ★ ☆ ☆ ☆ ☆   Instruction Card for Dominoes

Experiment until you can answer the following:

1. Using only the dominoes in this box, what is the length of the longest straight line of dominoes that can be toppled in one continuous motion?

2. What is the circumference of the smallest circle that can be toppled in one continuous motion? What is the diameter of that circle?

PROJECT 15 East Is East

Curriculum areas: science, social studies, language arts

There's freedom to make this a very literal or a more theoretical project: the student finds fifteen objects or concepts that were once united and are now divided, explaining briefly what might have happened had the division NOT occurred.

advertisement

East Is East

. . . and west is west and never the twain shall meet—unless, of course, you believe that opposites attract.

student instruction card

 Instruction Card for East Is East

Fill this box with fifteen objects (pictures are allowed) or concepts that were once united in some way but are now divided or separate.

For each object or concept, predict in three sentences or less what would have happened if the division or separation had *not* occurred.

PROJECT 16 Emergency

Curriculum areas: social studies, science, language arts

In this problem-solving exercise, the student invents creative, alternative uses for six everyday objects. Envisioning an emergency (or several different crisis situations), the student lists three ways each object could be used to help.

The items listed for inclusion in the box are readily found in variety stores and in many large supermarkets.

advertisement

Emergency

And you thought you had troubles!
Here's hoping you don't have any
trouble with this box.

student instruction card

Instruction Card for
Emergency

List three ways that each item in this box could be used to help you in an emergency.

Don't forget to name or describe the emergency: plane crash, hurricane, flood, toothache, or whatever. You may use each item for a different emergency if you wish.

PROJECT 17   The Good Ol' Days

Curriculum areas: social studies, art, science

The student identifies at least five out of ten drawings of unusual implements actually used in the past, then illustrates their use and redesigns one for future use in the vacuum of outer space.

To prepare the box, photocopy and cut apart the tool cards (pages 39-44) and select ten.

A list identifying the implements pictured on these tool cards is included on page 38 for your reference.

Materials to include in box for
THE GOOD OL' DAYS

☆ Instruction card.
☆ Ten tool cards.

---

advertisement

The Good Ol' Days

The objects pictured in this box date back to the good ol' days, when your grandfather chopped wood for his father before breakfast and then walked five miles to school, uphill, in freezing snow three feet deep, and NEVER complained. The least you can do is identify the pictures.

---

student instruction card

Instruction Card for
The Good Ol' Days

1. First identify at least five of the tools in this box. Then demonstrate all you know about them by creating an album of pictures that shows each tool being used in the good ol' days.

2. During the 1960s, scientists had to modify everyday conveniences to make them suitable for use by astronauts on a voyage to the moon. Suppose that the modern counterparts of the tools in this box had to be modified for space travel. Choose one and redesign it for use in the vacuum of outer space. You may either make a model of the redesigned item or create a picture and a written description.

PROJECT 17   The Good Ol' Days
Tool card answer key

The implements pictured on the tool cards are as follows:

1. Dress or skirt clip to raise the hem from muddy ground.
2. Tin force pump, used for whitewashing, cleaning, etc.
3. Blowing tube and poker for tending fire.
4. Potato peeler and slicer.
5. Copper cider muller, set upright in hot ashes.
6. Woodturner's sizing tool to gauge and maintain accuracy on later work.
7. Cooper's rim wedge.
8. Wooden loop used as a ring for tying animals.
9. Brass button polishing board.
10. Fruit jar sealer to insure a good seal between rubber ring and lid.
11. Pie lifter to remove hot pie from oven.
12. Tie block clamp for hauling natural ice from pond.

The Good Ol' Days
Tool Card 1

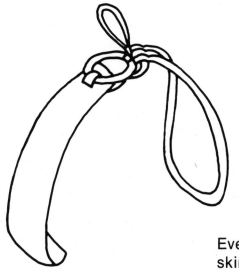

Even after Sir Walter Raleigh's day, long skirts and dresses were still the fashion. Could this have helped "milady" after a storm?

The Good Ol' Days
Tool Card 2

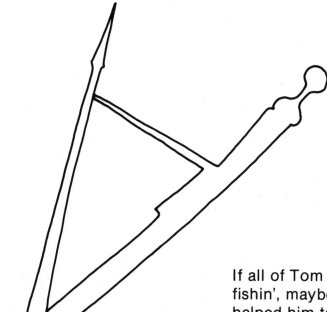

If all of Tom Sawyer's friends had gone fishin', maybe this gadget could have helped him to join them before the big ones got away.

Sometimes it takes more than wood
to keep the home fires burning.

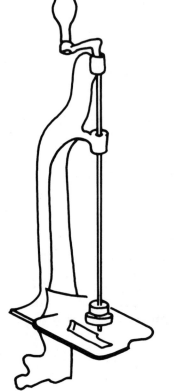

This may look like a workshop drill, but
it would more likely be found in a kitchen.

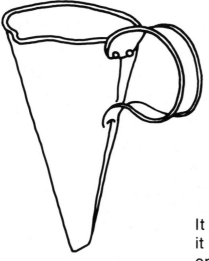

It may look like a megaphone, but instead it might help to warm you up after a walk on a cold winter's night.

It's an interesting woodworking tool that might have been used for marking, cutting, clamping, measuring, lifting, or turning. It is still used today by woodturners.

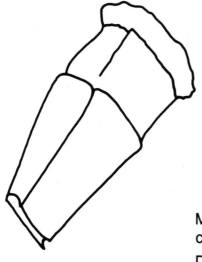

Most wedges were made for splitting or cutting. But note the concave edge.

Does it still have you over a barrel?
Who used this one?

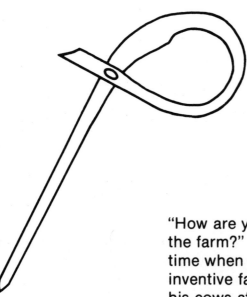

"How are you going to keep them down on the farm?" That was a good question at a time when iron was scarce. What was this inventive farmer's solution for keeping his cows at home?

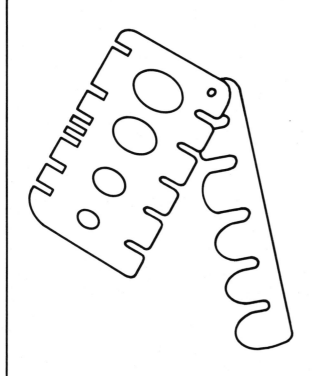

The Good Ol' Days
Tool Card 9

Tarnishing was a problem for the silver-smith, but that's not all. Tailors and dressmakers shared the dilemma. How could this gadget help?

The Good Ol' Days
Tool Card 10

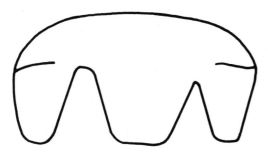

Too many tomatoes in your garden is no problem today if you have a freezer. But how could this kitchen gadget, which is small enough to hold in the palm of your hand, help to put August tomatoes in a January stew?

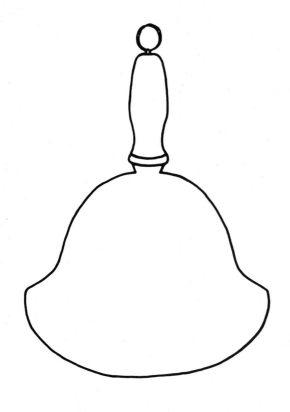

This could be a food chopper, a fan, or a paddle. But it's not. Instead, it might have been used early Sunday morning at home before dessert in the park.

Is it an andiron or an anchor? Absolutely not! But what connection could it possibly have with ice cream, lemonade, and chicken?

PROJECT 18   Habitat

Curriculum areas: science, reference skills

Any student who is not acquainted with his or her closest neighbors certainly will be after doing this project. The student must list every possible organism (at least thirty) that could be living within ten feet of the building in which he or she resides.

advertisement

Habitat

A woman's home is her castle, as the saying sometimes goes.

The question is, who else's castle is it?

student instruction card

☆ ☆ ☆ ☆ ☆ ☆ ☆ ☆ ☆ ☆ ☆   Instruction Card for Habitat

Imagine a line drawn on the ground outside the place where you live. The line is exactly ten feet away from the building at all points.

Make a list of every possible organism (name at least thirty) that *could* be residing inside or outside the structure, within the boundaries of the line.

PROJECT 19   Hour Glass

Curriculum areas: science, math, social studies, language arts

This timed (one hour) activity pushes the student to think quickly and break out of normal thought patterns in order to create four items (from a list of ten) using only paper, tape, and scissors.

advertisement

Hour Glass

Here's a one-hour race against time and frustration. You are armed with only paper, scissors, and tape.

On your mark, get set . . .

student instruction card

Instruction Card for
Hour Glass

Construct four of the items on the task card, using only the materials found in the box: paper, tape, and scissors.

You have just ONE HOUR to complete your work. You will receive extra credit for each additional item (beyond four) you are able to make within the time limit.

Hour Glass

How many of these can you make in one hour?

1. A life-saving device. (State the life-threatening situation and tell how the device would be used.)

2. A three-dimensional, imaginary animal with an unusual feature that would allow it to inhabit a polluted planet.

3. A device to measure the approximate height of a three-story building, accurate to within one foot.

4. An irrefutable clue to your identity.

5. A wasp trap.

6. A hearing aid.

7. A container that would hold a seven-pound rock.

8. A teaching aid to help young children understand simple subtraction problems.

9. A communication device.

10. A device that measures time.

Task Card

PROJECT 20   Ice Box

Curriculum areas: social studies, science

The student analyzes the effects of ice on mankind, identifying at least fifteen different effects and classifying them as positive or negative. The student then chooses one effect from each category as the most influential in human history and defends his or her choice in writing.

advertisement

Ice Box

Completing this box could be a chilling experience. Be prepared!

student instruction card

☆ ☆ ☆ ☆ ☆ ☆ ☆ ☆ ☆ ☆ ☆   Instruction Card for
Ice Box

Consider all the ways that ice has affected mankind.

1. List as many of these ways as you can. You must list at least fifteen ways.

2. Divide your list into two categories, using the chart in this box.

3. From each category, choose the effect that has most influenced the course of human events. Support your choices convincingly in writing.

Ice Box

Positive Effects of Ice	Negative Effects of Ice
1. _____	1. _____
2. _____	2. _____
3. _____	3. _____
4. _____	4. _____
5. _____	5. _____
6. _____	6. _____
7. _____	7. _____
8. _____	8. _____
9. _____	9. _____
10. _____	10. _____
11. _____	11. _____
12. _____	12. _____
13. _____	13. _____
14. _____	14. _____
15. _____	15. _____
16. _____	16. _____
17. _____	17. _____
18. _____	18. _____

PROJECT 21 I've Got a Secret

Curriculum area: social studies

How does secrecy affect the course of history? The student researches to find five historical secrets that, had they been found out, would have changed history as we know it. To qualify, each secret must have been known by someone at the time.

advertisement

I've Got a Secret

Can you keep a secret? What would happen if certain secrets weren't kept?

If you know the answer to the problem in this box, don't keep it a secret!

student instruction card

 Instruction Card for I've Got a Secret

Fill this box with five historical "secrets" (concepts, facts, or the like) that, had they been found out at a certain time in history, would have changed the course of human events.

There is only one restriction on the items you choose: Each named secret must have been known to someone, somewhere on earth, during the period when history could have been changed.

List each secret, describe the historical situation at the time, and explain how history might have been changed.

PROJECT 22   Kidnapped

Curriculum area: social studies

In this project the student explores cause and effect in history, naming one single person whose absence might have prevented the American Revolution, and explaining why.

advertisement

Kidnapped

"In 1492 Columbus sailed the ocean blue . . ."
But what if he hadn't?

You'll sail through this box if you're up-to-date
on your American history.

student instruction card

                                                    Instruction Card for
                                                    Kidnapped

It is the year 1770. Alien beings from another solar system secretly observe Earth and its inhabitants. They are greatly distressed by what they see. Their computers predict a major conflict between several small settlements on a large continent called America and a small but powerful island named England.

In order to do the Earthlings a favor, the space visitors decide to kidnap one person whose absence, they believe, will prevent the American Revolution from taking place in 1776.

Which person might they choose? Why? Document in writing the reasons for your choice.

PROJECT 23   King Kong

Curriculum areas: science, art

The student analyzes the special effects that film makers use in science fiction or horror films, trying to discover their secrets. The student then puts together a scene that could be photographed to create a similar illusion.

If you have a camera available, plan to photograph the scene according to the student's instructions, to test its effectiveness. Alternatively, encourage students to experiment with their own photography.

advertisement

King Kong

There's more to King Kong than meets the eye.

If you keep your eyes peeled for the tricks of his trade, this box should prove to be no problem.

student instruction card

Instruction Card for King Kong

Make a list of ten ways in which "seeing is believing" in a horror film or science fiction movie.

In other words, try to discover some of the secrets behind the special effects that the film producers use.

Then create a scene in this box that can be photographed to demonstrate one of these special effects. You may stipulate how the picture must be taken—in a dark room, at a certain angle, and so on. Come prepared for your creation to be photographed.

PROJECT 24 Know It All

Curriculum areas: language arts, math, social studies

Each Know It All task card presents fifteen "answers" consisting of numbers, words, and phrases. The student does research as needed to devise an appropriate question for each answer, wording each question so that the given phrase answers it exactly. There are, of course, many different questions that will work for a single answer.

Two sets of sample student answers, one for each task card, are included on pages 57-58 for your reference.

advertisement

Know It All

You may be good at finding answers, but how good are you at finding questions?

The answers are here. You provide the questions, and you'll know it all!

student instruction card

Instruction Card for
Know It All

Read the fifteen answers listed on the task card. Then, on the response sheet, write one question that could be answered with each of the items.

The answer given must be an *exact* response to the question you write.

Use your imagination and have fun!

Know It All

Here are the answers. What are the questions?

1. Splashed.
2. Alexander Pope.
3. An empty nest.
4. 1/3.
5. Melted jello.
6. In the middle.
7. Defrosting.
8. Hush puppies.
9. A popped balloon.
10. Peeling skin.
11. Increased humidity.
12. Busily.
13. Exploring outer space.
14. Lost.
15. More than 1/2.

Task Card A

Know It All

Here are the answers. What are the questions?

1. 10 decibels.
2. Less than 1/2.
3. 10,000.
4. 1972.
5. The tip.
6. Oysters Rockefeller.
7. Chitlins.
8. Accumulated wealth.
9. Let them eat cake.
10. Christopher Wren.
11. Assembly line production.
12. They put the wheel to work.
13. Writing limericks.
14. It's all relative.
15. Sincerely.

Task Card B

Know It All
Response Sheet

Just to prove I "know it all," here are the questions:

1. _____
_____

2. _____
_____

3. _____
_____

4. _____
_____

5. _____
_____

6. _____
_____

7. _____
_____

8. _____
_____

9. _____
_____

10. _____
_____

11. _____
_____

12. _____
_____

13. _____
_____

14. _____
_____

15. _____
_____

PROJECT 24   Know It All
Sample student answer

The sample below represents one student's ideas for Task Card A. This is for your reference only; it is NOT an answer key. Many other questions are possible for each answer.

TASK CARD A

1. *Splashed.*
   What is the past tense of the word splash?

2. *Alexander Pope.*
   Who was the English poet born in London on May 21, 1688?

3. *An empty nest.*
   What do you have when the birds fly away from home?

4. *1/3.*
   Solve: $9 \times 2 - 4 \div 7 \times 12 \div 8 \times 4$ What is the ratio of the number of this question and the answer of the problem, reduced?

5. *Melted jello.*
   What do you have left when you bake jello in the oven?

6. *In the middle.*
   Where is the hole in a doughnut?

7. *Defrosting.*
   What is your freezer doing when you unplug it or turn it off?

8. *Hush puppies.*
   What (is/are) the name of a kind of flavored soft ices, a kind of shoes, or what you would say if you wanted baby dogs to be quiet?

9. *A popped balloon.*
   What did Piglet give to Eeyore for his birthday?

10. *Peeling skin.*
    What is an after-effect of sunburn?

11. *Increased humidity.*
    What makes some people's hair go straight and others' go curly?

12. *Busily.*
    How do good students work on their projects?

13. *Exploring outer space.*
    What is every astronaut's goal?

14. *Lost.*
    Where are you when you don't know where you are?

15. *More than 1/2.*
    Is 3/4 more or less than 1/2?

—Wendy

PROJECT 24   Know It All
Sample student answer

The sample below represents one student's ideas for Task Card B. This is NOT an answer key. As with Task Card A, many different questions are appropriate for each answer.

TASK CARD B

1. *10 decibels.*
   What is the usual difference between the power output of a stereo speaker?

2. *Less than 1/2.*
   Is 1/4 more or less than 1/2?

3. *10,000.*
   What is 20,000 divided by 2?

4. *1972.*
   If I was born in 1966, what year was it when I was 6?

5. *The tip.*
   What is the last thing you give to a waitress before you leave a restaurant?

6. *Oysters Rockefeller.*
   What is a likely appetizer on the menu of an expensive restaurant? Or, what two things do you find at the beach in the summer?

7. *Chitlins.*
   What is another name for the intestines of a pig prepared as food?

8. *Accumulated wealth.*
   What's another name for saved wealth?

9. *Let them eat cake.*
   What were Marie Antoinette's famous words?

10. *Christopher Wren.*
    Who is a famous architect in England?

11. *Assembly line production.*
    How are teachers made?

12. *They put the wheel to work.*
    What did the cavemen do for mankind?

13. *Writing limericks.*
    How does a songwriter usually start out in his profession?

14. *It's all relative.*
    What is Albert Einstein's theory about relativity?

15. *Sincerely.*
    What is one method of concluding a letter?

—Nancy, grade 5

PROJECT 25   Let There Be Light

Curriculum areas: science, language arts

The student collects five pieces of evidence that light exists, writing a justification for each one.

Some of the evidence that students have successfully defended includes: television, a camera, a photograph, a telescope, a rainbow, a shadow, a leaf, a mirror, a firefly, a flashlight, a match, an eclipsed moon, a sun dial, an x-ray.

Materials to include in box for
LET THERE BE LIGHT

☆ *Instruction card.*

advertisement

Let There Be Light

Looking for an enLIGHTening experience?
You will see the light when you complete
this deLIGHTful box!

student instruction card

☆ ☆ ☆ ☆ ☆ ☆ ☆ ☆ ☆ ☆ ☆   Instruction Card for
Let There Be Light

Fill this box with five pieces of evidence that clearly demonstrate the existence of light.

Defend in writing each object you include in the box.

PROJECT 26   Man on Mars

Curriculum areas: science, social studies, language arts

Role-playing a geologist of the future on a manned flight to Mars, the student chooses the location for a colony, estimates distances, describes the greatest potential threat to life, and suggests what qualities would be desirable for the first inhabitants.

A geologic map of Mars (order #I-1083) can be purchased from the U.S. Geological Survey Branch of Distribution, 1200 South Eads Street, Arlington, VA 22202.

advertisement

Man on Mars

This box will send you into orbit if your map skills aren't up to par!

student instruction card

Instruction Card for
Man on Mars

You are the chief geologist on the first manned flight to the planet Mars. It is your responsibility to locate a site for a future space colony on the surface of the planet. You must also identify any possible threat to the safety of the first colonists.

Use the task card and map as you complete your important assignment.

Man on Mars

1. Pinpoint one or more places on the planet Mars where you feel a space colony could most suitably be located. Defend your recommendation using data you find on the map.

2. Approximately how long would it take an adult human being to walk from the center of the crater *Helmoltz* to the center of the crater *Volgel*? How did you estimate the distance?

3. Given the information provided on the map, describe the greatest threats to the humans who establish the first colony on Mars.

4. The first colony on Mars will support only ten people for ten years. Time and limited resources will prevent a return shuttle to Earth during the ten-year period. Assume that any of the ten people could pilot the spacecraft in addition to their other duties. What abilities, skills, and traits should these first ten colonists have?

Task Card

PROJECT 27   Meeting of the Minds

Curriculum areas: social studies, art, reference skills

Imagining a party attended by twenty diverse public figures, both past and present, the student assembles people who share a common interest into pairs or small groups, then creates a cartoonist's conception of the party scene and topics of conversation.

To prepare the box, photocopy and cut apart the guest name cards (pages 63-64).

Some suggested groupings are given on page 65 for your reference.

advertisement

Meeting of the Minds

You are throwing a party that is guaranteed to be a huge success—IF you invite the right people. Check this box out and celebrate!

student instruction card

 Instruction Card for Meeting of the Minds

You host a party one evening that gathers together many distinguished characters from both the past and the present.

The party is going well and these folks are all engrossed in conversation. As you pass among your guests, you realize that each pair or group is discussing a subject of common interest.

Use the guest name cards to arrange your guests in pairs or small groups. Then create a cartoonist's conception of the scene that evening. Be sure to indicate in some way the topic of conversation among each group of guests.

Meeting of the Minds Guest **John James Audubon**	Meeting of the Minds Guest **Sir James Barry**
Meeting of the Minds Guest **Rachel Carson**	Meeting of the Minds Guest **James E. Carter**
Meeting of the Minds Guest **George Washington Carver**	Meeting of the Minds Guest **John Chapman**
Meeting of the Minds Guest **Jacques Cousteau**	Meeting of the Minds Guest **Robin Hood**
Meeting of the Minds Guest **Elizabeth Kenny**	Meeting of the Minds Guest **Joyce Kilmer**

Meeting of the Minds Guest	Meeting of the Minds Guest
Ponce de León	**Herman Melville**
Meeting of the Minds Guest	Meeting of the Minds Guest
Sir Isaac Newton	**Georgia O'Keeffe**
Meeting of the Minds Guest	Meeting of the Minds Guest
Pablo Picasso	**Emily Post**
Meeting of the Minds Guest	Meeting of the Minds Guest
Sir Walter Raleigh	**John D. Rockefeller**
Meeting of the Minds Guest	Meeting of the Minds Guest
Franklin D. Roosevelt	**William Tell**

PROJECT 27   Meeting of the Minds
Sample answers

Below are some suggested groupings of the party guests and the topic of conversation for each group. Many others are possible; allow for student inventiveness.

1. Sir Walter Raleigh and Emily Post, discussing etiquette.
2. Franklin D. Roosevelt and Elizabeth Kenny, discussing polio.
3. John Chapman and Joyce Kilmer, discussing trees.
4. Herman Melville, Rachel Carson, and Jacques Cousteau, discussing ocean life.
5. Ponce de León and Sir James Barry, discussing eternal youth.
6. George Washington Carver and James E. Carter, discussing peanuts.
7. Pablo Picasso, Georgia O'Keeffe, and John James Audubon, discussing painting.
8. Robin Hood and John D. Rockefeller, discussing philanthropy.
9. Sir Isaac Newton and William Tell, discussing apples.

PROJECT 28   Mountains and Molehills

Curriculum areas: social studies, language arts

Getting problems in perspective—that's the task of the student who analyzes eight problems, classifies each one as a "mountain" or a "molehill," and explains the reasoning behind every decision.

To prepare the box, photocopy and cut apart the eight problem cards (pages 67-68). Copy the Mountains and Molehills emblems (page 69) and glue each on a separate manilla or brightly colored envelope.

advertisement

Mountains and Molehills

You can make mountains out of molehills or molehills out of mountains—it all depends on your point of view.

See if you can make molehills out of the mountains in this box.

student instruction card

☆ ☆ ☆ ☆ ☆ ☆ ☆ ☆ ☆ ☆   Instruction Card for
Mountains and Molehills

"Don't make mountains out of molehills," or so the saying goes. The problems in this box are either overwhelming "mountains" or manageable "molehills," depending on who and where you are.

Read each problem card and decide just how formidable the problem is. Then separate the cards into two groups, mountains and molehills. Describe on the back of each card the reasons for your decision. Place each group in the appropriate envelope.

Mountains and Molehills
Problem Card 1

You are a young girl, 17 years old, living in the United States in 1833. You have successfully completed your public schooling and would like to attend the same college where your brother is now studying.

Mountains and Molehills
Problem Card 2

You are a Basque living in northern Spain. You plan to migrate to the United States. Since your work is sheepherding, you are looking for similar employment in the United States.

Mountains and Molehills
Problem Card 3

The school party is tomorrow, and you promised to bake brownies. When you start collecting the ingredients, you find you have no unsweetened chocolate. It is too late to buy some because all the stores are closed. You are going to use the brownie recipe anyway and substitute something for the chocolate.

Mountains and Molehills
Problem Card 4

As a soldier with General George Washington at Valley Forge, Pennsylvania, in the winter of 1777, you are discouraged. The British have taken Philadelphia. Many of your fellow soldiers are dying of small pox. The supplies are inadequate. The weather is frigid. There is nothing to do to pass the time during the interminable winter. You miss your family in Rhode Island and want to write to them.

Mountains and Molehills
Problem Card 5

The Emancipation Proclamation of 1863 has declared all slaves living in the Confederate States to be free. You are living as a slave in the South, and now you want to leave your master and start your own farm.

Mountains and Molehills
Problem Card 6

Your friend arrives at your house excited. She has a new moped and asks if you would like to try it. While you are riding, you fall and scratch the bike. When you return and explain what happened, she laughs and says "Don't worry." You then discover that it isn't her moped, but that she took it without permission from a neighbor.

Mountains and Molehills
Problem Card 7

On December 5, 1945, the control tower of the Naval Air Station in Fort Lauderdale, Florida receives a radio message from a training flight. They report an emergency. They cannot see land and are not sure of their position. The plane vanishes. This same area today has been nicknamed the Bermuda Triangle. You are on a flight from Florida to Bermuda and will be forced to fly directly over the Triangle.

Mountains and Molehills
Problem Card 8

You are on a cross-country automobile race from Albany, New York to San Francisco, California. You are estimating a total of twelve days to complete the trip. You have $60 in cash. The year is 1907.

Mountains

Molehills

PROJECT 29   One If by Land . . .

Curriculum area: social studies

The student finds and describes ten famous signals used in history, then devises a secret signal to tell other students (without alerting the teacher) when the principal is out of the building.

advertisement

One If by Land...

Got your signals straight?
Try this box and find out!

student instruction card

Instruction Card for
One If by Land . . .

1. After a lantern signal was flashed in the steeple of Boston's Old North Church, Paul Revere rode through the night from Boston to Lexington to warn of the coming of British troops. Fill this box with ten more famous signals. Describe the situation in which each signal is (or was) used.

2. Devise a signal to indicate to your fellow students when the principal is out of your building. Your signal must be one that cannot be easily detected by teachers. Provide a written description of your signal and place it in an envelope in this box.

PROJECT 30 Out of This World

Curriculum areas: science, social studies, art

In this two-part project that stretches visual thinking skills, the student imagines and investigates what the earth would be like on a different topological surface. For the first part of the project, the student creates and analyzes a model of a doughnut-shaped earth. For the second part, the student depicts a sunset viewed from a particular point on that imaginary earth.

Materials to include in box for
OUT OF THIS WORLD

☆ Instruction card.
☆ One task card.

advertisement

Out of This World

Have you ever imagined a sunset that was simply "out of this world"?
This box will keep you going around in circles until you do.

student instruction card

Instruction Card for
Out of This World

Imagine that the earth is shaped like a large doughnut with a hole in the center. The size of the hole is equal to the diameter (distance across at the center) of the present earth.

With this image orbiting firmly in your mind, complete the two projects described on the task card.

Out of This World

Complete both of the following projects.

1. Make a three-dimensional model of the doughnut-shaped earth. Place each of the present earth's continents, oceans, and seas on the new planet.

   Could such a planet actually exist in our solar system? Why or why not? Write a page stating your scientific opinion.

2. Draw or paint a sunset as it would appear if you were a person living on the inner-ring surface of the doughnut-shaped earth. Be sure to pinpoint your position in relation to the setting sun.

Task Card

PROJECT 31   Paper Plates

Curriculum areas: social studies, science

The student imagines that disposable dinnerware is banned, and itemizes in chart form 25 changes that would occur as a direct or indirect result of that ban.

advertisement

Paper Plates

Whatever would we do without paper plates?
ContemPLATE this box and find out!

student instruction card

Instruction Card for Paper Plates

Conservation experts across the country recommend that paper goods and all disposable eating utensils (such as paper plates and paper cups) be banned. After much public debate, legislation is passed prohibiting the use of any disposable dinnerware.

You are a creative news analyst. Develop a chart on the enclosed paper plate to show the ramifications of the "paper-plate ban." Include at least 25 changes that would occur as a direct or indirect consequence of the new law.

PROJECT 32   The Queen's Jewels

Curriculum area: social studies

The student selects five objects that represent mankind's most important conceptual advances, then explains the idea symbolized by each one.

advertisement

The Queen's Jewels

What could be more precious than the queen's jewels?

Complete this box, and you'll be worth your weight in _____.

student instruction card

☆ ☆ ☆ ☆ ☆ ☆ ☆ ☆ ☆ ☆ ☆   Instruction Card for The Queen's Jewels

Fill this box with five objects that represent, in your opinion, the five most important concepts conceived by mankind. State the concept that each object represents. If you include an invention, you must state in writing the ideas behind the invention.

PROJECT 33 Quicker-Picker-Upper

Curriculum area: science

In this scientific experiment, the student tests at least five substances for absorbency, reports the methods and results of each experiment fully in writing, and fills the box with the most absorbent material found.

advertisement

student instruction card

Instruction Card for
Quicker-Picker-Upper

Fill this box with one cup of the most absorbent
material you can find. Before making your selection,
you must test the absorption power of at least
five different substances and report in writing
the methods you used for testing. Include the
results from each test.

PROJECT 34   Rubber Band

Curriculum area: science

What stretches besides a rubber band? The student's job here is to find 25 unrelated, stretchable materials, and to order them on a scale from most to least stretchable. Although rubber bands have varying elasticity, allow students to include only one per box.

A list of some of the objects students have collected appears on page 77 for your reference.

advertisement

Rubber Band

This may be stretching it a bit, but if you are good "down the stretch," this box should be no problem.

student instruction card

Instruction Card for
Rubber Band

Fill this box with at least 25 unrelated objects or materials that can be stretched. (Only one rubber band per box, please.)

Provide a list of the items you select, ranking them in order from the most stretchable to the least stretchable.

PROJECT 34 Rubber Band
Sample answers

Below is a selection of the many stretchable objects that students have included or listed for this project. Their ranking according to stretchability will vary depending on the particular item or piece of material the student has in the box.

1. Plastic.
2. Trick pencils.
3. Cotton fabric.
4. Aluminum foil.
5. Polyester fabric.
6. Elastic waistbands.
7. Foam rubber.
8. Crepe paper.
9. Saran wrap.
10. Coat hanger.
11. Straw.
12. Yarn.
13. Thread.
14. Garbage bags.
15. Tape measure.
16. Hair.
17. Fish net.
18. Leather.
19. Suede.
20. Nylon.
21. Band-Aids.
22. Gum.
23. Cotton balls.
24. Wet spaghetti.
25. The cornea in an eye.
26. A soap bubble.
27. A piece of taffy.
28. Shoelaces.
29. Popcorn kernels.
30. Silly Putty.
31. Licorice whips.
32. A balloon.
33. Human skin.
34. Scotch tape.
35. A piece of screen.
36. A mattress.
37. Wallpaper.
38. Typewriter ribbons.
39. Socks.
40. A penny on a train track.
41. Guitar strings.

PROJECT 35   Scavenger Hunt

Curriculum areas: reference skills, science, social studies

The student researches standard reference sources or invents creative means to locate the items listed on the task card. A student may not buy anything to complete this project. Task Cards A, B, and C emphasize scientific vocabulary plus some social studies research; Task Card D involves problems of change in both science and the social sciences.

Possible answers and back-up information for Task Cards A, B, and C are given on pages 81-82 for your reference.

advertisement

Scavenger Hunt

Scavengers would travel to the ends of the earth to collect bits of this, that, and the other.

There's no telling where you may have to go in search of the items in this box.

Happy hunting!

student instruction card

☆ ☆ ☆ ☆ ☆ ☆ ☆ ☆ ☆ ☆   Instruction Card for Scavenger Hunt

This will be a scavenger hunt you'll never forget!
Fill the box with the items on the task card.

Remember, a scavenger never buys anything.

Scavenger Hunt

Fill this box with the following items.

1. Mercenaria.
2. A keyhole limpet.
3. A picture of an Indian pachyderm.
4. A condensate.
5. A resonator.
6. A residuum.
7. A weak edible acid (be careful with this one).
8. A picture or sample of a syncarp.
9. A picture of a totipalmate cormorant.

Task Card A

Scavenger Hunt

Fill this box with the following items.

1. A metamorphic rock.
2. An object that would belong to a philatelist.
3. A list of ten items that were found in Tutankhamen's tomb.
4. A picture or model of the animal that supplies ambergris.
5. A skeleton of a microscopic animal.
6. The average age of the children of one-half of the teachers in your school.
7. A hybrid fruit.
8. A liter of air.
9. A dead cell.
10. A small amulet.
11. A map of a country that no longer exists.

Task Card B

Scavenger Hunt

Fill this box with the following items.

1. A suspected carcinogen.
2. A picture of the metatarsal arch.
3. A talisman.
4. The retail price in 1929 of a new Chevrolet Coupe without extras.
5. A picture of an animal that estivates.
6. The street address of the governor's residence in your state.
7. The name of the maternal grandmother of the president of the United States.
8. One of the front page headlines of the New York *Times* for September 14, 1943.
9. A picture of an Indian pachyderm.
10. A map of a country that no longer exists.

Task Card C

Scavenger Hunt

Fill this box with the following items.

1. A piece of matter that has changed form at least four times. List the changes.
2. An object capable of eliciting powerful emotions. State the emotions.
3. A model or picture of an item that increases in value when damaged or defective.
4. An object capable of changing the behavior of the largest number of people. Tell why.
5. An example of a non-mechanical object capable of measuring the longest period of time.
6. The smallest object that can cause things to be moved over the greatest distance.

Task Card D

PROJECT 35 Scavenger Hunt
Sample answers

The information that follows is a reference guide to the items student scavengers are asked to collect for Task Cards A, B, and C.

TASK CARD A

1. Mercenaria are shells, commonly called quahogs, which were used by some Native American tribes as a form of money.

2. A limpet is a small sea animal, related to the snail, that is found clinging to rocks in and around tide pools. (They are **not** barnacles.) A limpet's shell is shaped by its environment. The conical shell is high (more pointed) when the limpet is attached to a rock; it is low (flatter) when found in a deep, calm tide pool where the limpet does not have to fight the surf and air. A keyhole limpet is simply a type of limpet with a small keyhole-shaped opening at the top of the shell.

a limpet

3. The Indian pachyderm is an elephant with small ears close to the side of its head. (African elephants are bigger and have large, wide ears.)

4. A condensate is any substance that has been condensed; for example: evaporated milk, maple syrup, salt.

5. A resonator is any object capable of producing a series of regular vibrations; for example: a rubber band, a whistle, a musical instrument, a blade of grass.

6. A residuum is the substance that remains after a chemical process has taken place; for example: ashes after a fire, fat in the pan after frying bacon.

7. Any citrus fruit is a weak edible acid, as are hot peppers.

8. Grapes and raspberries are examples of syncarps.

9. A cormorant is a large fish-eating sea bird with webbed (totipalmate) feet.

TASK CARD B

1. Metamorphic rocks have undergone a pronounced change in structure caused by pressure, heat, and water, making them harder and more crystalline. Marble, quartz, and granite are examples of metamorphic rocks.

2. A philatelist is a stamp collector.

3. This list will vary with the student and the source of information. Ask the student to cite his or her source.

4. Ambergris is a waxy substance believed to originate in the intestines of the sperm whale. It is used in the manufacture of perfumes.

5. Coral is the horny skeleton deposited by tiny marine polyps.

6. Answers will vary. This item will have to be computed by individual schools.

7. A hybrid fruit is one derived from two different varieties or species; for example: a tangelo, a nectarine, a navel orange.

8. A closed liter-sized container contains a liter of air. A burning match may be inserted into the neck of the bottle to demonstrate the presence of air, although this is not necessary.

9. Examples of dead cells include a dead battery, a piece of dandruff, a piece of human hair.

10. An amulet is a charm or ornament used to protect the wearer against evil, disease, witchcraft, or bad luck. Almost any item used for such a purpose could be classified as an amulet.

11. Examples of countries that no longer exist (or have changed names) include Gaul, Persia, Ceylon, Parthia, Portuguese West Africa, Prussia.

TASK CARD C

1. A wide variety of answers are possible here. Do not discount any student's response without asking for supporting data. Some possible items are: a cigarette, diet cola or saccharin, peach pits, the sun, asbestos, cranberry sauce, age. (Yes, age itself has been identified a possible carcinogen!)

2. The metatarsal arch is the arch formed by the metatarsus bone of the primate foot. The metatarsus bone is the foot bone between the ankle and the toes.

3. A talisman is an object with an astrological sign or message engraved upon it, used to avert evil and bring good fortune.

4. $595.00, according to an advertisement in a 1929 *National Geographic* magazine that pictures the car and lists the price.

5. Estivation is characterized by a state of torpor or sluggishness with little or no motor activity and a generalized loss of sensation. In outward appearance, estivation resembles hibernation, but there are two major differences: (1) estivating animals do not experience the drastic drop in body temperature of hibernators, and (2) estivating animals often wake in the winter to feed while hibernators do not. (The body temperature of hibernating animals closely approximates the temperature of the environment, unless the outside temperature drops below freezing.) A bear is an example of an animal who estivates, while a chipmunk is a hibernator.

6. Answers will vary according to state and can be researched through a reference library.

7. Answer will change through successive presidencies.

8. The banner headline was "Bitter Battle Rages at Salerno; British Sweep Ahead in South; Bryansk is Stormed by Russians." Two other headlines on the front page were "Americans Under Fire in Italy" and "Allies Push Inland."

9. Same as Task Card A, item 3.

10. Same as Task Card B, item 11.

PROJECT 36 Shadow

Curriculum areas: science, language arts

The student investigates the way different objects obstruct light; finds or names objects that cast (or don't cast) shadows of varying size, shape, and color; and finally describes ten ways shadows benefit mankind.

advertisement

Shadow

Peter Pan had a real problem with his shadow before Wendy sewed it on for him.

If you can keep track of your own shadow (and a few others), you should have the shadow box all sewed up!

student instruction card

Instruction Card for Shadow

Fill this box with the following items.

1. The name of the object that casts the largest shadow you have ever seen.

2. An object capable of casting the most unusual shadow you can imagine.

3. An object that does not cast a shadow.

4. An object that casts a colored "shadow." Describe how this happens.

5. A single object that is capable of casting a triangular, a circular, and a square shadow.

6. A list of ten ways in which shadows are useful to mankind.

PROJECT 37 Shake, Rattle, and Roll

Curriculum areas: science, language arts

Focusing on the auditory sense, the student collects objects that can produce at least 35 distinct sounds, then writes phrases to describe the sounds, using a different adjective and noun for each one.

advertisement

Shake, Rattle, and Roll

Fill this box with creaking, scratching, and marching, and you will make the hit parade.

student instruction card

Instruction Card for
Shake, Rattle, and Roll

1. Fill this box with as many distinct sounds as you can. All of your sound-making equipment must be contained in the box. In order to complete this project, you must be able to produce at least 35 different sounds.

2. Make a list of the objects in the box and write a two-word description of the sound produced by each one. Your descriptive phrase must contain a different adjective and noun for each sound. For example:

    a propeller—a soft whirring
    a nickel—a loud clink

PROJECT 38 Signs of the Times

Curriculum areas: social studies, language arts

In this project the student is asked to take a broad view of the world of the 1980s, identifying and explaining the significance of five signs that typify our modern times.

Sample responses are shown on page 86 for your reference.

Materials to include in box for
SIGNS OF THE TIMES

☆ Instruction card.

advertisement

Signs of the Times

What is the signature of the times we live in? Try your eye at this box.

student instruction card

☆ ☆ ☆ ☆ ☆ ☆ ☆ ☆ ☆ ☆ ☆

Instruction Card for
Signs of the Times

Fill this box with five signs, any kind, that most clearly reflect the times in which you live.

Write a short paragraph about each sign you choose, describing its significance. That is, what does this sign tell you about the world *today* and the people who live in it?

PROJECT 38 Signs of the Times
Sample answers

Students might list a wide variety of signs for this project. Some have included the following ideas:

1. **No Littering**—reflects present-day environmental concerns; also reflects an affluent consumer society with many disposable goods.

2. **Speed Limit 55**—instituted because driving at slower speeds saves gasoline, this sign is a reminder of the limits of natural resources (i.e., oil) and our need to find new energy sources.

3. **Speed measured by radar**—reflects the use of advanced technology and the pervasive influence of the automobile.

4. **No nukes**—reflects the freedom of opinion in our society, and reflects growing public concern about the hazards of nuclear power as an energy source.

5. **McDonalds**—reflects a time in which people increasingly turn to the ease and convenience of fast-food outlets; also reflects the modern prevalence of business chains and franchises.

PROJECT 39   Spelling Bee

Curriculum area: language arts

*What patterns and idiosyncrasies make some words
harder to spell than others? That's something the student
must discover in coming up with twenty of the hardest
spelling words (up to fourteen letters long) in the English language. The student also finds a way to test the
difficulty of the list and reports the results of that test.*

advertisement

Spelling Bee

Here's a spellbinding activity—a chance
to put your teacher's spelling skills
to the test!

student instruction card

Instruction Card for
Spelling Bee

What makes a word hard to spell? Is it length, or is it
something else?

Construct a spelling word list for adults that contains,
in your judgment, twenty of the hardest words to spell
in the English language. No word on your list may be
longer than fourteen letters.

Devise a method to evaluate the difficulty of your test.
Report the results of your evaluation in writing and
include the report in this box with your spelling list.

PROJECT 40 Stairway to the Stars

Curriculum areas: science, reference skills

Researching to find the tallest (or longest) known member in 21 categories of living organisms, the student then arranges them in a "stairway," heeding two restrictions: that no natural enemies be on adjoining stairs, and that no organism be placed lower on the stairs than a heavier one.

To simplify the research for a lower level project, include the Guinness Book of World Records, which is available in paperback at most bookstores or from Bantam Books, Inc., 666 Fifth Avenue, New York, NY 10019.

A list of the tallest (or longest) organisms (Guinness Book of World Records, 1982) is given on page 90.

Materials to include in box for
STAIRWAY TO THE STARS

☆ Instruction card.
☆ One task card.
OPTIONAL *(lower level)*:
☆ Guinness Book of World Records.

advertisement

Stairway to the Stars

This may not be the quickest way up to the stars, but it certainly is a towering problem.

Are you UP to it?

student instruction card

Instruction Card for
Stairway to the Stars

Can you build a living stairway to the stars?
Complete the four activities on the task card.

Don't overlook the cautions!

Stairway to the Stars

1. Find the tallest (or longest) member of each of the following 21 categories.

   1. land mammals
   2. sea mammals
   3. humans
   4. birds
   5. reptiles
   6. amphibians
   7. fish
   8. arachnids
   9. crustaceans
   10. insects
   11. centipedes
   12. millipedes
   13. worms
   14. mollusks
   15. jellyfish
   16. extinct animals
   17. trees
   18. seaweed
   19. ferns
   20. grasses
   21. leaves

2. Arrange the members representing each category to form the longest possible "living ladder" to the stars.

   CAUTION: You may *not* place together on the stairway any animals who are natural enemies.

   CAUTION: You may not place any animal on the stairway below one of greater weight. (Squish!)

3. Compute the height of your stairway.

4. Make a scale model of your stairway.

Task Card

PROJECT 40 Stairway to the Stars
Answer Key

Following are the tallest (longest) members of each category as given in the 1982 edition of the Guinness Book of World Records. Note that this book is updated every year and that some answers may change in subsequent editions. Also, students may find different answers in other sources. Make allowances where students have good research to support their conclusions.

1. Land mammal: giraffe, 20 feet.
2. Sea mammal: blue or sulphur-bottom whale, 110 feet 2½ inches.
3. Human: Robert Pershing Wadlow, 8 feet 11 inches.
4. Bird: long-tailed fowl or onagadori, with tail feathers 34 feet 9½ inches.
5. Reptile: reticulated python, 32 feet 9½ inches.
6. Amphibian: Chinese giant salamander, 5 feet.
7. Fish: whale-shark, 60 feet 9 inches.
8. Arachnid: South American "bird-eating" spider, leg span 10 inches.
9. Crustacean: giant spider crab, claw span 12 feet 1½ inches.
10. Insect: Indonesian stick-insect, 13 inches.
11. Centipede: *Scolopendra morsitans*, 13 inches.
12. Millipede: *Graphidostreptus gigas* and *Scaphistostreptus seychellarum*, 11.02 inches.
13. Worm: ribbon worm or "boot-lace" worm, more than 180 feet.
14. Mollusk: giant squid, 57 feet.
15. Jellyfish: cnidarian Arctic giant jellyfish, tentacles stretching to 120 feet.
16. Extinct animal: diplodocus, 87 feet 6 inches.
17. Tree: coast redwood, 366.2 feet.
18. Seaweed: Pacific giant kelp, 196 feet.
19. Fern: tree-fern, 60 feet.
20. Grass: Bermuda grass, "Callie" hybrid, 18 feet.
21. Leaf: raffia palm and Amazonian bamboo palm, 65 feet.

PROJECT 41   A Sticky Situation

Curriculum areas: science, language arts

After reading a brief, factual account of the Boston "molasses flood" of 1919, the student chooses one of two activities: in the first, the student writes descriptions of this or similar cleanup operations as they would proceed in the years 1919, 1983, and 2083; in the second, the student performs and later describes experiments to rank ten liquids (including molasses) according to viscosity.

The optional book, Danger, Disasters, and Other Horrid Deeds, at 5th-6th grade readability, contains an eyewitness-style account of the Boston molasses flood. It is available in hardcover or paperback from Yankee Inc. Books, Dublin, NH 03444.

advertisement

A Sticky Situation

Without some stick-to-itiveness and a flood of creative solutions, completing this box may land you in some sticky situations.

student instruction card

Instruction Card for
A Sticky Situation

Read the following historical report and choose *one* of the two task cards to complete this box.

On January 15, 1919, twenty-one men, women, and children died when an eight-foot tidal wave of molasses swept through the streets of Boston, Massachusetts. The disaster occurred when a holding tank 58 feet high ruptured, emitting a stream of syrupy molasses under a pressure of two tons per square foot. Freight cars were washed away, buildings collapsed, and underground offices were filled with the bubbling liquid. Molasses reached a depth of five feet above street level in certain areas. It was weeks before the devastated area could be cleaned up.

A Sticky Situation

You are in charge of street cleanup operations for the Boston molasses flood. Describe each step in your plan to clean up the sticky mess. Include any equipment and materials you will use. (Remember, it is 1919.) Estimate the manpower and time needed to complete the job.

The year is 1983. The same disaster occurs. What changes would you make in your cleanup operations?

The year is 2083. Use your imagination to predict a future cleanup operation for a similar substance. You may invent any machinery that you feel would be helpful in getting the job done.

Task Card A

A Sticky Situation

The resistance of a gas or liquid to flowing, or the property by which it resists a change in shape, is called *viscosity*. The viscosity of liquids depends on how quickly the molecules in the fluid can slip past each other. Molasses is a more viscous fluid than cooking oil.

Select ten viscous liquids (one should be molasses) and rank them in order from the *most* to the *least* viscous. Describe the tests you used to determine the viscosity of each liquid in relation to the others on the list.

Task Card B

For duplication

PROJECT 42   Story Problems

Curriculum areas: math, language arts

Working backwards from four given answers, the student writes a humorous story problem for each one, including at least three mathematical steps that result in the answer.

One creative student response for answer number 3 is included on page 94 for your reference.

advertisement

Story Problems

In this box you'll find several problems and no stories. You should have no problem with this box, however, if you are a good storyteller.

student instruction card

Instruction Card for
Story Problems

On the task card in this box, you will find four answers to math story problems. But what were the stories, and what were the problems?

You must create a humorous story to accompany each answer. Each story must have *at least three mathematical steps* that result in the given solution.

Story Problems

Math story problem answers:

1. 7,241 broken pencil sharpeners

2. 16¾ inches of frayed nylon rope

3. 342 gallons of lukewarm fudge sauce

4. 72.6 Swedish meatballs

Task Card

PROJECT 42   Story Problems
Sample student answer

Here is the problem one student submitted for answer #3.

Al's Ice Cream Shoppe received an order for 22,188 ounces of fudge sauce from a wealthy banker. The banker wanted to treat all of the bank's depositors to hot fudge sundaes to celebrate the bicentennial of the bank's opening. When Al received the order he nearly fainted, but a job is a job. Al started in on the order. When he had almost completed cooking the sauce, the banker called again. He needed 10,794 more ounces of fudge sauce. Al did faint this time. After four days of making nothing but fudge sauce, Al was exhausted. Just as he was about to funnel the last drop into a container, the banker's secretary called. "We've underestimated the sauce we'll be needing. Double that last order." Al dragged his body back to the stove.

When Al finally finished the job, he called to arrange delivery at the bank. "What fudge sauce?" the bank manager asked. "No one here ordered any fudge sauce. Someone must have been playing a joke on you."

How many gallons of lukewarm fudge sauce did Al have? If he charged $9.99 per gallon, how much money had he lost on the deal?

22,188 ounces + 10,794 ounces = 32,982 ounces

32,982 ounces + 10,794 ounces = 43,776 ounces

43,776 ounces ÷ 128 ounces = **342 gallons of sauce**

342 gallons × $9.99 per gallon = $3416.58 loss

—Jim, grade 7

PROJECT 43   The Test of Time

Curriculum areas: social studies, reference skills

Which of our cultural artifacts have stood the test of time for the last 300 years? And what items that we use today will likely last another 300 years? The student lists and collects ten items in each category and must be prepared to defend each one.

To prepare the box, photocopy and cut apart the two Test of Time lists on page 96. Obtain two large Zip-loc plastic bags and enclose one list in each.

advertisement

The Test of Time

You'll have this box in the bag if you can find ten 300-year-old antiques.

student instruction card

Instruction Card for
The Test of Time

Can you recognize true staying power when you see it?
What products of our civilization can stand the test of time?

You'll find two bags in this box. There is a list in each bag. Fill one of the bags with ten items that are familiar to most people in our country today and would also have been familiar to people who lived 300 or more years ago.

Fill the other bag with ten items from this century (1900-2000) that you feel people 300 years from now will still readily recognize.

Be prepared to discuss and defend each item you include.

The Test of Time

Things Familiar Now and
Three Hundred Years Ago

1. _____

2. _____

3. _____

4. _____

5. _____

6. _____

7. _____

8. _____

9. _____

10. _____

The Test of Time

Things Familiar Now and
Three Hundred Years From Now

1. _____

2. _____

3. _____

3. _____

5. _____

6. _____

7. _____

8. _____

9. _____

10. _____

PROJECT 44 Toothpaste

Curriculum areas: science, language arts

The student uses scientific research techniques while performing tests and making comparisons of three competitive brands of toothpaste. In a follow-up report, the student describes the tests and their results in writing and ranks the three products in each of three categories.

Toothpaste is readily available in supermarkets and pharmacies. Other brands may be substituted for those listed.

advertisement

Toothpaste

Put your money where your mouth is!

You'll be "ULTRA-BRITE" if you can complete this box.

student instruction card

Instruction Card for Toothpaste

1. Test and compare the three brands of toothpaste in this box for any three of the following:

   abrasiveness

   fluoride content

   irritation

   bacteria-killing ability

   whitening ability

   taste

   cost

2. Describe each test in writing and include the results.

3. Use the enclosed form to rank each toothpaste according to the results of your tests.

Toothpaste
Data Collection Form

Notes	3 (High)	2 (Average)	1 (Low)
Abrasiveness			
Fluoride content			
Irritation			
Bacteria-killing ability			
Whitening ability			
Taste			
Cost			

PROJECT 45   UFO

Curriculum area: language arts

In this exercise in critical analysis, the student reads three eyewitness reports of UFO sightings and is asked to judge the reliability of each report. The student is encouraged to formulate questions he or she might ask in an interview with the eyewitnesses, questions that would help in making the evaluation.

One sample student response is included on page 105 for your reference.

advertisement

UFO

Real or imagined?

Examine the evidence presented here and take a stand!

student instruction card

☆ ☆ ☆ ☆ ☆ ☆ ☆ ☆ ☆ ☆   Instruction Card for
UFO

As the chief officer in charge of investigating reports of unidentified flying objects, you have received the three percipient reports enclosed in this box. It is your job to evaluate the reports and to classify them as possible, improbable, or impossible, based on the information given and any other information you may find.

State the reasons for your decisions in one page or less. Also, assuming you could interview the percipients, what are the most important questions you would ask about each incident? In other words, what information would you like to have in order to make a better decision?

DEPARTMENT OF UFOLOGY

PERCIPIENT REPORT
FOR
UFO SIGHTING

PERCIPIENT: _____Capt. Carlos Rodriguez_____

Name (Please print or type.)

DATE: _____November 11, 1979_____

PLACE: _____Over the island of Ibiza, Spain_____

TIME: _____Approximately 2200 hours_____

WEATHER CONDITIONS: _____Clear_____

CATEGORY (PLEASE CHECK ONE):

_____ Encounter: Observation of UFO and occupant(s).

_____ Boarding: Percipient taken on board UFO.

___X___ Sighting: Observation of lights, shapes, unusual radar reading.

_____ Contact: Interaction between UFO and object on Earth. No

occupant(s) observed.

OTHER WITNESSES: _____None_____

ACCOUNT OF SIGHTING: (Be as specific as possible.)

I was piloting a Caravelle jetliner on a routine flight to Tenerife in the Canary Islands when I saw four flying spheres. They were bright red in color and three times larger than a star or shooting spark. These spheres pursued the aircraft for four hours. At this point, I decided that the safety of my aircraft and passengers was in jeopardy. Therefore, I decided to abort the flight. The objects peeled out of sight 30 miles from Valencia. I was able to make a safe emergency landing at Valencia with no injury caused to any passengers or crew.

These simulated percipient reports are based on incidents reported by real people whose names have been changed for the purposes of this project.

DEPARTMENT OF UFOLOGY

PERCIPIENT REPORT
FOR
UFO SIGHTING

PERCIPIENT: _____Anne and Albert Morgan_____

Name (Please print or type.)

DATE: _____19 September 1961_____

PLACE: ___New Hampshire, U.S.A._____

TIME: ____Approximately 2300 hours_____

WEATHER CONDITIONS: ___Clear_____

CATEGORY (PLEASE CHECK ONE):

___X___ Encounter: Observation of UFO and occupant(s).

___X___ Boarding: Percipient taken on board UFO.

_____ Sighting: Observation of lights, shapes, unusual radar reading.

_____ Contact: Interaction between UFO and object on Earth. No

occupant(s) observed.

OTHER WITNESSES: ___None_____

ACCOUNT OF SIGHTING: (Be as specific as possible.)

We were driving home from a vacation in Canada and decided to drive all night to reach our home near Boston. At about 11:00 P.M., when we were driving through the hills of New Hampshire, we saw an object in the sky. We first thought it was an aircraft or a satellite. It appeared to be following us; then it hovered very close to us. When we stopped the car, it stopped too. Albert got out of the car and walked across the field to within 50 feet of the object. We could clearly see the shape. It was not a satellite or an aircraft, but rather a large, pancake-shaped, solid vehicle with fin-like projections on each side. It had a row of windows and was lit from within. We could see several figures inside. One of the figures definitely appeared to be the leader. The vehicle came even lower to the ground, and what looked like a ladder was lowered beneath it. At this point Albert ran back to the car and we drove away very fast. Then we heard a beeping noise and saw the lights again. The lights and the beeping noise followed us as we drove on home. We realized when we got home that the trip had taken us at least two hours longer than it should have. We have no recollection of stopping anywhere after seeing the UFO, nor do we have any real memory of the road we took afterwards.

Several weeks after our experience, we were still very upset about what we had both seen. We decided that perhaps hypnosis sessions would alleviate our continued anxiety. We were hypnotized separately, not knowing the outcome of each other's sessions. Under hypnosis, we both related a very similar account of what happened after Albert got back into the car.

Apparently we drove on, but turned onto a side road where we came upon a group of figures standing in the road. We stopped, got out of the car, and were led away into the woods. The UFO was on the ground now. We were taken inside, laid on a table, and given a medical inspection. We were then led back to our car and told to drive away.

DEPARTMENT OF UFOLOGY

PERCIPIENT REPORT
FOR
UFO SIGHTING

PERCIPIENT: ____Jake McNeely_____

Name (Please print or type.)

DATE: ____August 21-22, 1955_____

PLACE: ____McNeely Farm, Kelly, Kentucky, U.S.A._____

TIME: ____Approximately 1900 to 0330 hours_____

WEATHER CONDITIONS: ____Clear_____

CATEGORY (PLEASE CHECK ONE):

___X___ Encounter: Observation of UFO and occupant(s).

_____ Boarding: Percipient taken on board UFO.

_____ Sighting: Observation of lights, shapes, unusual radar reading.

_____ Contact: Interaction between UFO and object on Earth. No

occupant(s) observed.

OTHER WITNESSES: ____Buck Johnson and 12 members of the McNeely family____

ACCOUNT OF SIGHTING: (Be as specific as possible.)

Buck Johnson was at the farm visiting us on the evening of August 21. We were playing cards in the kitchen. Buck went outside to get a drink of water from the well at about 7:00 P.M. (We have electricity at the farm, but no running water and only a fireplace for heat.) Buck came running back to the house saying that he had seen a flying saucer land behind the house. We laughed and told him it must have been a shooting star. About an hour later our dog, Wolf, started barking. I looked out as Wolf ran away and hid under the tractor next to the barn. I saw a strange light coming toward me out of the darkness. As the light came closer, I could see that it was a little man. He was about 39 inches tall and he was shining. His head was too big for his body and his arms were too long. He had hands like a bird's claw, his eyes were huge and looked like two flashlights, and he had on a funny silver suit. It sounds crazy, but that's what I saw. He had his arms raised over his head as if to say, "I give up." He didn't look like any man I have ever seen. Buck and I grabbed our guns and started shooting. By now this creature was 20 feet from us. He did a somersault and disappeared into the darkness. Buck and I went back into the house and sat down. We could not believe what had just happened. Wolf was still outside hiding. We were just about to get back to our card game when I saw another creature looking through the window. Buck saw it too. He grabbed his gun, which was by his side, and

These simulated percipient reports are based on incidents reported by real people whose names have been changed for the purposes of this project.

fired it through the screen. We heard nothing, but we decided to go outside and look around. As I stepped out the door, one of the creatures reached down from the roof and touched my head. My friend, Buck, shot at it and knocked it off the roof onto the other side. Now we could see them everywhere. One was in a tree and one came from around the corner of the house. We shot at them all and this seemed to drive them away. When we thought we had hit them, it sounded like a bullet hitting a tin bucket. They would fall down and roll into a little ball.

Believe me, after 3 hours of this, we were all terrified. The decision was made to drive 7 miles into Hopkinsville and report all of this to the police. The police returned to Kelly with us to see for themselves. When we arrived back home, there were no signs of the creatures anywhere, only the holes in the screens and the cartridge casings on the ground. Having searched with no success, the police left about 2 A.M.

We all went to bed to try to sleep and forget what had happened. But at 3:30 A.M. I heard my mother scream. I grabbed my gun and ran to her bedroom where I saw one of the creatures staring at us through the window. I fired and the creature vanished. We haven't seen anything like it since and I hope we never do again.

PROJECT 45   UFO
Sample student answer

The sample below is one student's response to the percipient reports. As student ideas may vary considerably, this should not be considered an answer key.

Case #147 Jake McNeely
I think case #147 is improbable because the police found no evidence of alien beings landing anywhere near the McNeely home. To make a better decision, I'd like to know how the aliens felt (Jake McNeely said he was touched on the head), and I would like a picture of the alien.

Case #491 Anne and Albert Morgan
I think case #491 is most possible because they went under hypnosis separately and told a very similar report of the lost 2 hours. To make a better decision, I would like to know what the aliens looked like.

Case #2872 Capt. Carlos Rodriguez
In my opinion, case #2872 is very improbable because there were no witnesses and no one else noticed the objects. To make a better decision, I would like to know if any other planes were in the area at 2200 and if he, Captain Carlos Rodriguez, usually wears glasses but didn't wear them on that flight.

—Mark

PROJECT 46 Umwelt

Curriculum areas: art, science

The student first reads to learn about the way different animals' and insects' senses work, then recreates a natural scene as it would be perceived by three different creatures.

The View from the Oak: The Private Worlds of Other Creatures, by Judith and Herbert Kohl, is available in paperback through your local bookstore or from Charles Scribner's Sons, 597 Fifth Avenue, New York, NY 10017.

The three natural scenes should show varied terrain, vegetation, and inhabitants. Many good photographs can be found in old National Geographics or in natural history magazines.

advertisement

Umwelt

What do you look like to a frog?

How would a snake find its way through your classroom?

What in the world is an Umwelt?

Be the first on your block to know with this box.

student instruction card

Instruction Card for Umwelt

Read the book in this box, *The View from the Oak,* which describes in detail how animals other than man perceive the world.

Choose three animals whose sensory capabilities are described in this book; then recreate artistically any one of the three pictures enclosed in the box, showing the scene as it would appear to each of those three animals.

PROJECT 47 Water Clock

Curriculum areas: science, language arts

The student invents a water clock, writes the directions for its use, and suggests when it might be more useful than a regular watch or clock.

advertisement

Water Clock

If you can measure time in inches and water in minutes, then you should finish this box in no time!

student instruction card

☆ ☆ ☆ ☆ ☆ ☆ ☆ ☆ ☆ ☆   Instruction Card for
Water Clock

1. Devise a method to measure an hour of time with water.

2. Write a set of directions for using the device.

3. Describe three situations in which your water clock would be more useful than a conventional timepiece.

PROJECT 48   Where in the World

Curriculum areas: social studies, reference skills

The task card describes fifteen places or types of places ("a center of ancient worshop"), most suggesting more than one possible location. The student identifies a site for each description and locates the fifteen sites on world maps.

Consumable maps (desk size 8″ × 10½″) of the eastern continents (order #9D7) and the western continents (order #9D8) can be purchased in envelopes of 50 or bundles of 500 from Nystrom, 3333 Elston Avenue, Chicago, IL 60618.

One set of sample student answers is included on page 110 for your reference.

advertisement

Where in the World

Phileas Fogg went around the world in 80 days.

With the help of this box, your trip should be much shorter.

student instruction card

Instruction Card for Where in the World

Using the maps in the box, mark a dot at the location of fifteen places as listed on the task card. Label each location with its name and some indication of its significance.

You will need more than an atlas to locate these places. Don't forget to use your imagination, too!

Where in the World

Locate the following on your maps:

1. A place that connotes intense emotion.
2. A center of ancient worship.
3. The site of a national disaster.
4. The site of an international disaster.
5. The location of an ancient icon.
6. The location of a technological wonder.
7. A place of extreme wealth.
8. A place of aesthetic beauty.
9. The birthplace of a controversial hero.
10. The birthplace of a famous handicapped person.
11. The location of the first navel orange tree.
12. The site of an alleged UFO encounter.
13. The birthplace of a folk hero.
14. The winter home of the monarch butterfly.
15. A place of great superstition.

Task Card

PROJECT 48   Where in the World
Sample student answer

The sample below lists the places one student located on her set of maps. Many different answers are possible; this is NOT an answer key.

1. *A place that connotes intense emotion.*
   Iran (seizure of American embassy with hostages)

2. *A center of ancient worship.*
   Athens

3. *The site of a national disaster.*
   Texas (oil spill)

4. *The site of an international disaster.*
   Korea (Korean War)

5. *The location of an ancient icon.*
   Rome (Sistine Chapel)

6. *The location of a technological wonder.*
   Panama (the canal)

7. *A place of extreme wealth.*
   French Riviera along the Mediterranean

8. *A place of aesthetic beauty.*
   Grand Canyon, Arizona

9. *The birthplace of a controversial hero.*
   Omaha, Nebraska (Malcolm X)

10. *The birthplace of a famous handicapped person.*
    Alabama (Helen Keller)

11. *The location of the first navel orange tree.*
    Riverside, California

12. *The site of an alleged UFO encounter.*
    Death Valley, California

13. *The birthplace of a folk hero.*
    Massachusetts (Johnny Appleseed)

14. *The winter home of the monarch butterfly.*
    near the Gulf of Mexico

15. *A place of great superstition.*
    Egypt (ancient kings' tombs in pyramids)

—Lynn

PROJECT 49   Wonder Blob

Curriculum areas: science, social studies, language arts

Combining imagination, knowledge of the world, and a sense of how historians and archaeologists recreate past civilizations, the student invents a scientific report from the perspective of 3000 years in the future. The subject? What can be learned about the primitive civilization of the late 1900s from this priceless artifact: a Silly Putty egg.

Silly Putty is available in most toy and variety stores.

A sample student response is included on page 112 for your reference.

Materials to include in box for
WONDER BLOB

☆ *Instruction card.*
☆ *One Silly Putty egg.*

---

advertisement

Wonder Blob

It's a bird! It's a plane! It's WONDER BLOB!

But what in the world is it?
Only time will tell.

---

student instruction card

   Instruction Card for
Wonder Blob

Three thousand years from now, civilized beings on the planet Earth are excavating along the ancient shoreline of the Atlantic Ocean. One group of diggers discovers the small oval object in this box.

Since so little data is available on the primitive civilizations of the 1980s, this discovery is immediately hailed throughout the scientific community as a major find.

After a period of intensive study, one of the great minds of the future reports to the world about the fragile beings who inhabited Earth at the end of the twentieth century.

You are that great mind of the future. Write a scientific report listing at least ten of your major findings about the ancient civilization, based on the material in this box. (You must, of course, return this priceless artifact in perfect condition, since it will be displayed in a place of highest honor.)

PROJECT 49   Wonder Blob
Sample student answer

The sample below represents one student's ideas; it is NOT an answer key.

I, the Great Mind of the Future, hereby claim that the blob I have discovered shows that the people of the 1980s were:

1. . . . an industrialized civilization. The blob is found to be combustible, proving that it was used as a fuel.

2. . . . non-conservationists. People in the 1980s must have run out of resources because they did not recycle. Investigation of the blob shows no evidence of reprocessing.

3. . . . non-ecological. Many of the disposable plastics (the blob is classified as a plastic petroleum product) create problems of garbage disposal.

4. . . . chemists. In order to mix the chemicals that produced the blob, the people of the late twentieth century must have achieved a great deal of sophistication in the field of chemistry.

5. . . . miners. The blob shows evidence of petroleum, which geological records from that time indicate was found deep in the earth's crust.

6. . . . people who enjoyed amusements. The blob bounces and was probably a source of entertainment.

7. . . . a cooperative society. In order to produce or manufacture the blob, the people of the late 1980s must have been involved in reciprocal services.

8. . . . a technological society. There were obviously standardized procedures for producing the blob.

9. . . . a creative society consisting of inventors. In order to produce the blob, these people were required to turn raw materials of simple forms into complex materials.

10. . . . explorers and possibly seamen. Some of the materials in the blob were not available on the Atlantic coast. They either traveled to acquire this material or they traded with others.

11. . . . a society with a well-developed sense of humor. The blob was obviously planted by a member of the ancient civilization in an attempt to mislead a member of the future such as I. As is evident from my report, however, they were totally unsuccessful.

This concludes my report on the 1980s.

—Jim, grade 6

PROJECT 50 Zip-Loc

Curriculum areas: social studies, science

The student draws on historical, social, and scientific knowledge in collecting twelve containers (or pictures or models of containers) that meet the criteria described on the task card.

A selection of creative student answers is included on page 114 for your reference.

advertisement

Zip-Loc

You will hardly be able to CONTAIN yourself when this box is signed, sealed, and delivered.

student instruction card

Instruction Card for
Zip-Loc

Zip-loc bags are modern, all-purpose containers that come in many different sizes. They can hold anything from carrots to cassette tapes to seashell collections. What other sorts of containers do you know about?

Fill this box with the twelve types of containers listed on the task card. You may use pictures or models of the required items if necessary.

Zip-Loc

When you have completed this project, this box should contain the following:

1. The name of the oldest container.
2. The largest container that can hold water.
3. A container of containers.
4. The most valuable natural (not man-made) container.
5. The most valuable man-made container.
6. A natural container that is potentially harmful to people.
7. A container of historical significance.
8. An infamous container.
9. An edible container.
10. A container that can arouse intense emotions in people.
11. A container that can save a life. (The container itself must save the life, not the contents of the container.)
12. A container that can withstand intense pressure.

Task Card

PROJECT 50   Zip-Loc
Sample student answers

Following are some of the most creative answers that students have submitted.

1. The universe; the earth.
2. Ocean.
3. Bag of unshelled peanuts; any fruit (contains seeds, which contain the germ of life).
4. Skin.
5. Fort Knox.
6. Lakes; poisonous seeds.
7. Tutankhamen's tomb; the Eagle lunar landing module.
8. Jesse James's holster; atomic bomb.
9. Pie crust; ice cream cone (minus ice cream).
10. Telegram; envelope; casket; bullet shell.
11. Sleeping bag; boat; asbestos suit for a fire fighter.
12. Bathysphere.

MATERIALS TO PURCHASE

PROJECT	MATERIALS	WHERE AVAILABLE
All projects	Rainbow Boxes for project storage, sold in sets of 6 or 30.	Dale Seymour Publications, P.O. Box 10888, Palo Alto, CA 94303.
1. Airplane	One balsa airplane.	Variety store or toy stores.
	The Great International Paper Airplane Book by Jerry Mander, George Dipple, and Howard Gossage.	Bookstore or Simon and Schuster, 1230 Avenue of the Americas, New York, NY 10020.
2. At Your Convenience	One small flashlight, one container suntan lotion, one match, one pair of Polaroid sunglasses, one battery, one light bulb.	Variety store.
6. Big Mac	Five styrofoam hamburger boxes.	McDonalds (or another fast-food outlet with similar containers).
10. Bubble Box	Option for lower level: one heavy-duty 6-8 inch balloon, one jar of soap bubbles, 24 inches of 1-inch plastic tubing.	Variety store.
11. Clandestine	Pop bottle cap, aluminum foil.	Supermarket.
14. Dominoes	Box of 48 or more dominoes.	Toy or department store.
16. Emergency	Choose six of the following: rope (any length), 4 feet of 12-inch aluminum foil, two styrofoam cups, one pillowcase, one sponge, one spoon, one paper plate.	Variety store or supermarket.
19. Hour Glass	Paper, tape, scissors.	Variety store.
26. Man on Mars	Geologic map of Mars (I-1083).	U.S. Geological Survey Branch of Distribution, 1200 South Eads Street, Arlington, VA 22202.
31. Paper Plates	One paper plate.	Supermarket or variety store.
34. Rubber Band	One rubber band.	Variety store.
40. Stairway to the Stars	*Guinness Book of World Records.*	Bookstore or Bantam Books, Inc., 666 Fifth Avenue, New York, NY 10019.
41. A Sticky Situation	Optional: *Danger, Disasters, and Other Horrid Deeds.*	Yankee Inc. Books, Dublin, NH 03444.
43. The Test of Time	Two large plastic Zip-loc bags.	Supermarket or variety store.

PROJECT	MATERIALS	WHERE AVAILABLE
44. Toothpaste	Three tubes of toothpaste, different brands.	Supermarket or pharmacy.
46. Umwelt	*The View from the Oak* by Judith and Herbert Kohl.	Bookstore or Charles Scribner's Sons, 597 Fifth Avenue, New York, NY 10017.
48. Where in the World	Maps of the eastern continents (9D7) and the western continents (9D8).	School supply store or A. J. Nystrom, 333 Elston Avenue, Chicago, IL 60618.
49. Wonder Blob	One Silly Putty egg.	Toy or variety store.

THE WANT ADS

Which challenge do you want to take?

Mark off each box as you complete it.

1. AIRPLANE
It flies through the air with the greatest of ease. Or does it? Let your imagination "take off" on a new plane!

2. AT YOUR CONVENIENCE
These modern conveniences could be gone forever . . . unless YOU can remember how they worked.

3. AUDUBON
This box is for the birds, and for you, too, if you like your friends fine and feathered.

4. BELIEVE IT OR NOT
Six of one, half a dozen of another. You have at least a 50 percent chance of completing this box!

5. BIG FOOT
Would you go camping alone in the wilds of Northern California and Oregon? Try this box, then decide.

6. BIG MAC
Next time you have a Big Mac attack, save the box! It could come in handy in an emergency.

7. BONES
Some animals fly, some hang by their tails, some peel bananas. Mix up their bones, and what do you get?

8. BOOMERANG
Do you sometimes find yourself running in circles? This box may come back to haunt you!

9. BORING
Feeling bored? This box is a sure cure for the doldrums. Or is it? As Einstein said, it's all relative.

10. BUBBLE BOX
Lawrence Welk is forever blowing bubbles. You will be, too, if you can complete this box!

11. CLANDESTINE
DISCover how to DISCretely disguise an alien spacecraft without getting DISCouraged.

12. COKE MACHINE
What happens when you put the money in? We put in the questions, you dispense the answers.

13. COLORBLIND
Have you ever touched a rainbow? You will if you can get the feel for this "hands on" project.

14. DOMINOES
The Domino Theory: if the first one falls, so do the rest. Will the ones in this box work on that theory?

15. EAST IS EAST
. . . and west is west and never the twain shall meet . . . unless you believe that opposites attract.

16. EMERGENCY
And you thought you had problems! Here's hoping you don't have trouble with this box.

17. THE GOOD OL' DAYS
That's when children got up at 4 A.M. and walked to school in freezing snow . . . But what else did people do?

18. HABITAT
A woman's home is her castle, as the saying sometimes goes. The question is, who else's castle is it?

19. HOUR GLASS
Here's a one-hour race against time and frustration. On your mark, get set . . .

20. ICE BOX
Completing this box could be a chilling experience. Be prepared!

21. I'VE GOT A SECRET
Can you keep a secret? What if certain secrets weren't kept? If you complete this box, don't keep it a secret!

22. KIDNAPPED
"In 1492 Columbus sailed the ocean blue . . ." But what if he hadn't? See if you're up-to-date on your American history.

23. KING KONG
There's more to King Kong than meets the eye. Keep your eyes peeled for the tricks of his trade!

24. KNOW IT ALL
You may know all the answers, but what about the questions? The answers are all here . . . YOU decide what to ask.

25. LET THERE BE LIGHT
Looking for an enLIGHTening experience? You'll see the light when you complete this deLIGHTful box.

26. MAN ON MARS

This box will send you into orbit if your map skills aren't up to par!

27. MEETING OF THE MINDS

You're throwing a party that's sure to be a success . . . IF you invite the right people. Do this box and celebrate!

28. MOUNTAINS & MOLEHILLS

It all depends on your point of view. See if you can make molehills out of the mountains in this box.

29. ONE IF BY LAND . . .

Got your signals straight? Try this box and find out!

30. OUT OF THIS WORLD

Imagine a sunset that's simply out of this world. This box will keep you going around in circles until you do.

31. PAPER PLATES

What would we ever do without paper plates? ContemPLATE this box and find out.

32. THE QUEEN'S JEWELS

What could be more precious than the queen's jewels? Do this box and you'll be worth your weight in _____ .

33. QUICKER-PICKER-UPPER

Is it a vacuum cleaner, an anteater, or a school bus? You can really get absorbed in this activity!

34. RUBBER BAND

This may be stretching it a bit, but if you are good "down the stretch," this box will be no problem.

35. SCAVENGER HUNT

There's no telling where you may have to go in search of the items in this box. Happy hunting!

36. SHADOW

Peter Pan had a real problem with his shadow until Wendy sewed it on. Can you get this shadow box all sewed up?

37. SHAKE, RATTLE, AND ROLL

Fill this box with creaking, scratching, and marching, and you will make the hit parade.

38. SIGNS OF THE TIMES

What is the signature of the times we live in? Try your eye at this box.

39. SPELLING BEE

Here's a spellbinding activity; a chance to put your teacher's spelling skills to the test!

40. STAIRWAY TO THE STARS

This may not be the quickest way to the stars, but it's a towering problem. Are you UP to it?

41. A STICKY SITUATION

Without stick-to-itiveness and a flood of creativity, this box may land you in some sticky situations.

42. STORY PROBLEMS

You should have no problem with this box if you can tell a good story!

43. THE TEST OF TIME

You'll have this box in the bag if you can find ten 300-year-old antiques.

44. TOOTHPASTE

Put your money where your mouth is! You'll be "ULTRA-BRITE" if you can complete this box.

45. UFO

Real or imagined? Examine the evidence presented here and take a stand!

46. UMWELT

What do you look like to a frog? What in the world is an Umwelt? Be the first on your block to know with this box.

47. WATER CLOCK

If you can measure time in inches and water in minutes, you should finish this box in no time!

48. WHERE IN THE WORLD

Phileas Fogg went around the world in 80 days. With this box, your trip should be much shorter.

49. WONDER BLOB

It's a bird! It's a plane! It's Wonder Blob! But what in the world is it? Only time will tell.

50. ZIP-LOC

You will hardly be able to contain yourself when this box is signed, sealed, and delivered.

Certificate of Independent Study

This is to certify that

_____

has completed a program of independent study

at _____ School,

the _____ day of _____, 19 _____ .

Signed, _____

Design a Challenge Box

This is your big chance to ask the questions!

Create your own Challenge Box, using your intelligence and your imagination. There are only three rules to follow.

1. Design a box that is challenging.
2. Design a box that has more than one "correct" answer or product.
3. Design a box that does not require expensive materials.

Don't forget to include written instructions for others to follow when they try your box. You must also suggest some answers or finished products for your box.

Write an advertisement to interest other people in doing your box. Make the ad intriguing without giving away the whole project.

SAMPLE INTRODUCTORY LETTER TO PARENTS

Dear Parents:

This year I am working with a program called "Challenge Boxes," which is designed to promote creative and productive thinking skills.

The Challenge Boxes program works in three steps. Step One, "Completing a Box," is based on a set of fifty projects, stored in colorful boxes that the students can check out. Each box contains one or more challenging problems for the student to solve independently. These problems focus on higher level thinking skills and lead the students into creative and productive thinking in a variety of curriculum areas—science, language arts, math, social studies, art, and reference skills.

Students are sometimes required to "invent" a new item, or to evaluate an object with an eye to improving on it. Many boxes ask students to analyze data and to draw conclusions based on their analysis.

One box, for example, is called "Umwelt" (a term used to describe the world around a living creature as that creature, and *only* that creature, experiences it). The student finds in the box a book, *The View from the Oak,* which discusses the sensory capabilities of a wide variety of animals. After reading the book, the student must analyze the information and *apply* it by redrawing a natural scene (also included in the box) as it would appear to three different animals.

Step Two of the program, "Follow-up Discussion," involves adult-led group discussions among students who have successfully completed the same box. This experience of listening and responding to the ideas of others is an important part of the Challenge Boxes program.

Step Three, "Independent Study Project," provides for intensive individual or small group study based on the student's interest and achievement at Step One. At this stage, students may be encouraged to create their own boxes on themes of special interest to them—boxes that can then be shared with other children in the school.

I will be using the Challenge Boxes as part of my regular classroom curriculum. Students who show interest and ability in the boxes I present in class (and who regularly complete their classroom work) will be encouraged to check out a Challenge Box on their own. They are to work on these projects in school after finishing their other work, and may also take them home to work on.

Once a student begins to check out boxes, that child's involvement in Steps Two and Three of the program will depend on his or her performance at Step One.

Please contact me if you would prefer that your child not participate, or if you have any questions.

Sincerely,

SAMPLE FOLLOW-UP LETTER TO PARENTS

Dear Parents:

This is your child's first experience with an independent activity in the Challenge Boxes program. A letter describing the program was sent home with your child earlier. If you did not receive that description, please let me know and I will send another copy home.

I would like to invite you to participate with your child in this Challenge Boxes program. I encourage the students to ask you or any other person for helpful information. This is *not* considered "cheating" in this program. One of the best ways to obtain information is to ask someone who might know the answer—or at least might be able to suggest where the student could look to find it.

The following guidelines may be helpful as you work with your child on an activity:

1. Don't expect to know all the answers. Most of the projects in these boxes are quite difficult. The most important parent ingredients in the program are the willingness to discuss the problem with your child and the encouragement you can give.

2. Do realize that your involvement in this program is voluntary! Don't be manipulated into doing the whole project. The problem in the box belongs to your child.

3. Do let your child work with another if they both choose to. When the box is turned in, I will record it as a "partner box."

4. Do have fun! Also, please let me know about the strengths and weaknesses of the program from your point of view.

If you have any questions about the Challenge Boxes program and your involvement in it, please feel free to contact me.

Sincerely,